TAKE A DEEP BREATH

a comprehensive guide to the working
of the singer's voice

Henry Cummings

Thames Publishing
London

© 1993 Norah Cummings

The text and music examples of this book are copyright and must not be reproduced in any form, in whole or in part, without written permission from the publisher.

ISBN 0 905210 96 4

Printed by Hobbs the Printers of Southampton

CONTENTS

Acknowledgements		*page*	4
Introduction			7

Part 1 The human voice as a musical instrument

Chapter 1	Construction of the thorax	9
Chapter 2	Motive power of the voice and the muscles employed in breathing	11
Chapter 3	Construction of the larynx	18
Chapter 4	'Registers' and 'tessitura'	22
Chapter 5	Resonation	27
Chapter 6	Diction – the making of words and their enunciation	31

Part 2 Observations on the techniques of singing

Chapter 7	Phonation	53
Chapter 8	Breath control and legato singing	59
Chapter 9	Phrasing	62
Chapter 10	Agility	65
Chapter 11	Blending of the registers	70
Chapter 12	Good total production	79

Part 3 General advice

Chapter 13	'What type of voice do I have?'	89
Chapter 14	'Rest' – the danger of overwork	92
Chapter 15	Advice on the discovery of 'a voice'	93
Chapter 16	'How does it go?' – the study and approach to performing	95
Chapter 17	Repertoire	103

To my dearest Norah

*and to all my students,
from whom I learnt so much*

ACKNOWLEDGEMENTS

There are so many kind people who have helped with this book. I would like to give special thanks to Sir Thomas Armstrong; Sir Charles Groves; Yvonne Minton; Mr L M Naidoo; Mrs M Sutton, SRN, SCM, Hon FLCM; Dr S Pickford; Winston Ku; Mark Wildman; Margaret Thomas.

From SIR THOMAS ARMSTRONG

I had had many discussions with Henry Cummings about this book, and followed its progress with close interest. I could see that it was going to be a valuable help to many people, teachers as well as students and practising singers.

Henry Cummings had had wide experience as a performing artist, a teacher at The Royal Academy and elsewhere, and a discerning adjudicator. His insight into the problems of young singers was exceptional, and the fruits of his experience, together with his knowledge of the mechanics of the voice and of the problems of technique and style, will surely make his book an invaluable help to many people.

From SIR CHARLES GROVES, CBE

I worked with Henry Cummings on many occasions over the years and with several of his pupils. His great experience and success, both as a performer and also as a teacher, qualify him eminently to write a book intended for students who need to know everything about singing, and one intended to help teachers when preparing students for examinations. The title of the book, *Take a deep breath*, and the clear and unfussy chapter headings whet the appetite for a very readable and informative experience.

From YVONNE MINTON, CBE, Hon RAM

I have read *Take a deep breath* with great interest and I hope that it will reach a wide audience.

It is a profound study of the art of using the human voice, particularly as it affects singers, and would be invaluable to serious students of singing and to the teaching profession.

One of the attractions of the book is that it has obviously been written by someone who was able to combine a great knowledge of teaching with a lifetime of personal experience as a singer.

INTRODUCTION

The earliest recollection I have of my introduction to singing was the direction, so often repeated, 'Take a deep breath!'

I soon learnt the reason for this instruction as it was quickly demonstrated to me that the control of respiration (the intake and exhalation of breath) was possibly the most important aspect in the establishment of good singing technique.

The use of the voice as a musical instrument cannot be likened to that of others which are tangible and visual. Its development is made possible by highly organised and disciplined training of certain muscular parts of the body which, in everyday life, are not necessarily called upon to function with such precision and control as are demanded in the act of singing.

The voice is controlled by the will to perceive and experience the sensations of musical sound, which emanate from those parts of the body concerned with voice production, namely the muscular actions of breath control, those which govern pitch, resonance and tonal quality, and the enunciation of words. The brain is capable of developing what can be called another sense and which could be termed 'the singing sense'.

At times one has heard the sweeping statement 'singing just comes naturally', but there is much more to it than that. It is true that every good singer gives that impression, and it is also true that some voices show more natural aptitude than others in the early stages of training. However, just as athletes must undergo intensive mental and physical training to enable them to engage in feats of endurance which would not be attempted by 'the man in the street', so must would-be singers undergo such training to ensure the correct development of the muscular actions employed in the art of singing. What then emerges as 'just comes naturally' is the result of conscious study in the practise of the techniques of voice production, and it is by undertaking such training that the quality called 'natural' is accomplished. To quote Sir Adrian Boult, 'An object of the technique of all arts is the achievement of the desired end with the greatest simplicity and economy of means.'

INTRODUCTION

This book is intended as a guide to the understanding of the working of the human voice, when it is used as a musical instrument. It may also prove useful to anyone undertaking examinations in voice production, where such knowledge is a stated requirement.

However, obviously it is impossible to expect that by the possession of such knowledge gained only by book learning, one automatically becomes an accomplished singer. Certainly it would be very dangerous, and possibly harmful to the voice, to approach singing entirely on just a scientific basis. Singing is an art which embraces all one's emotions and mental and physical attributes — one's very soul and spirit.

On the subject of instruction, the writer will go so far as to say it is impossible to *teach* any of the arts. However, it is nevertheless necessary that study is undertaken with accomplished singers who have experienced all these emotions in actual performing and are therefore able to pass on such knowledge to receptive students who will eventually develop, using the knowledge passed on to them, the art of singing.

The individuality of temperament and vocal talent of each student necessitates close contact with the professor on a one-to-one basis, assuming that it is impossible to apply one rule to every student.

In addition, one must be judicious and not attempt to copy in one's own singing *vocal* attributes admired in others. Damage can result from trying to imitate or 'take on' another's vocal personality. Be conscious of your own vocal scope in its various stages of development, and do not try to force into it qualities that are not as yet present in your vocal individuality. Your voice must always be *you*; never try to make it sound like that of someone whose singing you admire but whose general qualities are quite different from those of your own.

Part 1 of this book consists of a detailed explanation of the component parts that go to make up the instrument, and a full description of its construction. Part 2 is devoted to suggested methods that may be used in the development of the technique of singing. Lastly, Part 3 includes discussions on some general aspects of the art of singing, including interpretation and repertoire, which I hope will be of interest and help, especially to young singers.

PART 1

THE HUMAN VOICE AS A MUSICAL INSTRUMENT

CHAPTER ONE

Construction of the thorax (chest cavity)

The construction of the THORAX has often been likened to a circular birdcage: the SPINAL COLUMN (the back bone) forming the upright stay at the back; the STERNUM (the breast bone) forming the upright stay in the front; and the RIBS, of which there are 12 pairs, forming the rungs which encircle the cage. The CLAVICLE (the collar-bone) forms the top of the cage, and the DIAPHRAGM, the most important muscle of the human body after the heart, forms the floor of the cage. The diaphragm is the main muscle used in breathing and it, together with other muscles concerned in respiration, will be dealt with in a later section. As far as the contents of the thorax are concerned, it is, at present, only necessary to mention the main organs therein: (1) the heart, the most important organ in the body; (2) the lungs, two light spongy elastic structures, somewhat pear-shaped, that will contain the air we use in breathing.

The rungs of the cage consist of 12 pairs of ribs which are, as mentioned above, positioned all the way round the chest. They vary in size, being shorter at the top, so that the overall shape is somewhat like that of a cone, with the lower sets of ribs spreading out at the base of the chest.

Counting down from the top of the cage near the collar bone the ribs are numbered as follows:

1) TRUE RIBS. The first seven pairs are termed TRUE RIBS. They are hinged to the backbone and attached by cartilage in front to the sides of the breast bone. Being so attached front and back, it will be

appreciated that their movement is limited to elevation during inspiration, expanding the chest in a front-to-back direction.

2a) FALSE RIBS. The FALSE RIBS are the remaining five pairs. The eighth, ninth and tenth are hinged to the back bone but are not attached in the front to the breast bone. They have attachment to each other by cartilaginous bands. This being the case, these three pairs have considerably more ability to move and enlarge the chest cavity from side to side and from front to back. In doing so the space at the base of the chest becomes greater.

2b) FLOATING RIBS. The last two pairs (the eleventh and twelfth) are termed FLOATING RIBS. They are small and are attached only to the spine and have no frontal movement.

CHAPTER TWO

Motive power of the voice and the muscles employed in breathing

MOTIVE POWER – The bow is the motive power in stringed instruments of the violin family. When it is drawn across the strings, sound is produced by their vibrating. (Motive power: the bow. Vibrating element: the strings.) Wind is the motive power in woodwind instruments and the reeds the vibrators. Certain woodwind instruments, namely oboes and bassoons, have doubled reeds, and there is a similarity to their action in creating sound in the vocal instrument, the voice. Here air is again the motive power and the vocal cords (a better name is 'vocal folds', as will be seen later, when their action will be fully described) the vibrating element. Sound is created by their vibration as the air passes between them. The muscles employed in breathing are the INTERCOSTALS, the DIAPHRAGM and ABDOMINAL muscles.

INHALATION and EXHALATION – By enlarging the thoracic cavity (the chest or ribcage), atmospheric pressure brings about the inrush of air into the lungs through the nose and/or mouth. In singing, one should always draw in the breath via the mouth. It ensures a good supply of air in a short space of time. However, during long interludes one may, if one wishes, take air in through the nose. In some cases it may be found relaxing and refreshing.

INHALATION – The ribs are supplied with muscles. There are 11 pairs, running from the first to the eleventh sets of ribs, positioned on either side of the rib cage. They are called the OUTER and INNER INTERCOSTAL muscles. When the outer set is brought into action, by contraction, the space in the chest is enlarged from front to back by elevation of the ribs. Combined with this action is the contraction of the DIAPHRAGM. This is the most important breathing muscle.

It is situated at the base of the rib cage, approximately at the waistline. It is attached at the back to the spine. In crossing the spinal column internally it has two extensions, one on each side of the third lumbar vertebral body. These extensions are called the CRURA (meaning legs) of the diaphragm. The diaphragm is attached all the way round the chest to the lower ribs and to the base of the breast bone in the front. It forms the floor of the thorax, and the roof of the abdomen, so separating those two compartments of the body. In its relaxed state it is dome-shaped, to some extent resembling a pudding basin placed on its rim, with the apex reaching up into the rib cage. When it is contracted, it descends into the upper abdomen, which is directly beneath it, and flattens out at the base of the ribcage. It will be seen that in this movement the space in the chest cavity is made greater from top to the bottom, and that the space at its base is also enlarged.

A bulge will now be felt around the waistline area, due to the downward pressure of the contracting diaphragm, which will now resemble, to some extent, that of a soup plate placed upside down. This contraction should be felt in the whole circumference of the body, right round the base of the chest from the front, under the cartilaginous ends of the false ribs, to the base of the spine at the back, where the floating ribs are attached. Perhaps one can more easily feel the bulge by placing the fingers just under the base of the breast bone, and panting in and out. There should now be the contraction of the upper muscular wall of the abdomen felt in an upward direction, making the top part of the abdomen firm enough to support the diaphragm's descent, thus ensuring that it is not forced down into the lower part of the abdomen and so displacing the organs therein. We now consider the lungs to be filled.

EXHALATION is effected by the elastic recoil of the lungs and chest wall, and by the action of the abdominal muscles pushing back the displaced abdominal contents underneath the relaxed diaphragm to resume its dome-like shape. The main abdominal muscles may be mentioned here. These are the flank muscles, TRANSVERSUS ABDOMINIS, which run round the sides of the abdomen, attached to the lower border of the ribs in front and the pelvis on each side, and the RECTUS ABDOMINIS, which run from the ribs to the groin on each side of the navel. The inner intercostal muscles are now also brought into action, controlled by the relaxation of the outer intercostal muscles, so ensuring a smooth outflow of breath.

This type of breathing is known as DIAPHRAGMATIC and INTERCOSTAL breathing, which ensures a good supply of air, and the control of compression. It is the correct method to employ for proper breathing, whether you are a singer or not.

There are other forms of breathing which are not good, either for health or for singing. CLAVICULAR breathing is where the air enters only into the narrow upper parts of the lungs, where the space of the rib-cage is small and very limited in movement for enlargement. This type of breathing uses muscles attached to the neck and skull and therefore would interfere with the muscles of the larynx and hence the control of the voice. The main nerve supply to the diaphragm is by phrenic nerves, which arise from the spinal cord in the neck as the cervical nerve-roots: three, four and five. There is a mnemonic which goes 'three, four and five, keep the diaphragm alive'. Added evidence why a singer should not use the neck muscles as in clavicular breathing: this is close to distress breathing, as in asthma and over-exertion. It indicates that the diaphragm is not being fully used. The tone produced is very shallow and unsupported and weak in quality. An obvious sign of this type of breathing is that of a raising of the shoulders on inhalation. ABDOMINAL breathing is caused by the fact that the diaphragm is allowed to press down, with too much force into the abdomen, owing to lack of support from the abdominal muscles. In this form of breathing the rib-cage does not have the necessary elevation to ensure space enlargement by expansion at its base. This results in the tone of the sound being very forced and ponderous, and lacking the vitality and the 'floating' quality associated with good voice production. An obvious physical sign of this type of breathing is that of a flat chest and protruding abdomen.

At this point advice must be given, especially to those in the early stages of training. When taking in a breath we must not over-do our efforts and take in more air than we can reasonably control. This fault can lead to complications and take up a lot of valuable time in undoing them later on. This is a fault often occurring in beginners. There is a temptation to take in so much air on inhalation that it is impossible to control it with the necessary restraint on exhalation. The pressure that has now been made on the intake is so great that it will be felt necessary to relax at once and get rid of the compression that has been built up. As this happens the muscles of control suddenly collapse, and the breath shoots out with no means of checking it.

There are two parts to the sudden collapse of muscular control:

1. The mechanical nature of over-inhalation, due to muscles pulling on the ribs, rendering difficult the control of untrained muscles.

2. The biochemical nature of the breathing, due to excessive oxygen or hyperventilation, leading to sudden cessation of breathing and lung collapse.

We must now consider the tremendous CONTROL OF THE BREATH TECHNIQUE called for in respiration in singing. This control is dependant, to a great extent, on the acts of COMPRESSION and SUPPRESSION, together with the other necessary muscular actions. It is considered necessary to be a little more technical at this point to ensure full understanding of the means by which air enters and leaves the lungs.

Normal breathing is basically involuntary, that is to say it is under the control of the respiratory centre in the brain. This is why we can breathe when we are asleep. There is also some control via the autonomic nervous system, which has a sort of monitoring control of the apparently involuntary functions of the whole body, including respiration. The autonomic nervous system is parallel to the central nervous system, which controls most voluntary functions. When the carbon-dioxide in the blood reaches a certain level, the nerves which control the diaphragm and intercostal muscles are triggered off to open the chest and allow atmospheric pressure to push air into the lungs. The more we can control diaphragmatic and intercostal muscles, the better our control of the air going into and out of our lungs.

It is quite a natural, subconscious action for us to 'take a breath' in the ordinary way of life – we have to do so to stay alive. We just take a breath as necessary. Sometimes the intake is sudden; at other times it is taken slowly through the nose or mouth. But as for breathing out, this is often haphazard and uncontrolled. Certainly word-phrasing is often not considered at all in our general approach to talking. At times we even *hold* the breath we take in, and then let it out again in a sudden burst, or expel it in a drawn-out sigh.

The use of the breath as the motive power in singing must, of course, be approached in a very different and highly considered manner.

It is necessary to use the actions of COMPRESSION and SUPPRESSION, and to balance them accordingly as required by the difference of pitch.

When the air has entered the lungs by the voluntary (or controlled) actions of the muscles of inhalation, as in voice production whether for singing or speaking on the stage, it becomes necessary to make the action of compression to send it out again. This is brought about by the diaphragm moving in an upward direction by controlled relaxation, also thereby lowering the lower ribs and reducing chest capacity in a lateral and front-to-back direction, so pressing out the air from the base of the lungs. At the same time the contraction of the inner intercostal muscles causes the compression in a lateral direction. (Here again is an example of diaphragmatic and intercostal breathing.)

Now follows the all-important act of controlled exhalation.
Unless there is some act of restraint brought about, the air will simply rush out with no control whatsoever. To obtain the perfect control of the outflowing breath, which is absolutely essential to negotiate the big demands of musical and word phrasing, we must make the act of suppression. This is to use restraint on the out-going breath, the stream of air on which we sing. This restraint is made by the action of the outer intercostal muscles to oppose the inward pull of the inner intercostal muscles as they contract to press out the breath by a lateral movement of the rib cage. At the same time, together with the action of the rib muscles, the abdominal muscles contract to control the upward movement of the diaphragm.

It is obvious that these actions of press and restraint will need adjustments in balance when the alterations of pitch occur in the music. In the lower regions of the overall compass of the voice, the pressure of breath will be relatively less than that required in the higher portions. The vocal folds will not offer great resistance in the lower pitches, but their tension will be increased as the higher pitches are reached. The various pitches of certain sections of the overall compass of the voice are classified in groups. A full explanation of the groupings and the reason for them, together with the method of their use, will be given in Chapter 4, 'Registers' and 'tessitura'.

At this juncture it must be stressed that the actions of both compression and suppression must take place only by the use of the breathing muscles. *Never* must the vocal folds be used as a means of resistance, in a 'gripping' fashion in the throat. This would result in grave damage, to say the least, and if allowed to persist could eventually completely ruin the voice. Whilst the voice *might* last for a time, insecure intonation would result. By too much force at the vocal folds or lack of the adjusted fold tensions, sharp or flat singing would result.

DYNAMIC/TONAL VOLUME – The variations in the intensity of tonal levels are made possible by both physical means and emotional desire. Various controlled pressures of breath are used to determine the increases and decreases in the amplitude of vibrations of the vocal folds which will produce dynamic levels from 'pp' to 'ff' as demanded, ie, loud note, large breath pressure; soft note, small breath pressure.

Combined with this must be the emotional desire on the part of the singer to give full expression in his interpretation of the words and the music.

ANTAGONIST MUSCLES – Some muscles are arranged in pairs and act in an antagonistic fashion, one contracting and the other relaxing. The action of both the contracting and relaxing muscles is of equal importance to enable controlled movements. Any acts made by antagonistic muscles must be co-ordinated and considered as an entire act and not that of an *individual* muscular act. This is necessary to ensure precision. As far as the carrying out of any *function* is concerned, there can be no isolated action of a single muscle. Some such antagonistic muscles are used in the act of breathing, others to control the adjustments of the vocal folds, as will be seen later.

So now, having a basic knowledge from a singer's viewpoint of the construction of the thorax, and the physiology of breathing, we turn to the matter which should, of course, be emphasized from the very beginning of training.

POSTURE is of the utmost importance in breathing correctly. On inhalation, certain intercostal muscular actions are made and the diaphragm contracts and commences its descent. The abdominal muscles contract in an upward and inward direction; they are 'tucked in' to give support and control to the centre of the diaphragm as it

MOTIVE POWER OF THE VOICE AND THE MUSCLES

contracts and raises and widens the ribcage. At the same time, the muscles of the buttocks should be contracted. They are called the GLUTEAL MUSCLES. These actions will ensure a firm base for diaphragm and rib movement.

Our body is our instrument and, as in the case of all other instruments, it must be held and positioned correctly. The way in which one stands is of paramount importance to ensure control. One must also remember that good appearance is essential when on the stage or platform. Nobody wants to see a drooping singer or one looking tense and rigid in performance. One needs to convey authority and involvement, and this can be shown very considerably in the way one stands. Find the most comfortable position for the feet and, in doing so, feel quite secure and balanced. A good position to adopt is that with the feet slightly apart, with one foot a little forward. One must leave the hands free and not let them, or the fingers, fidget. One should not beat time with any part of the body and not use elbows when drawing in the breath, etc. One should just try to show relaxation and ease. So, 1) stand in an upright position, raise the head, and imagine it being suspended from above, but remembering not to raise the shoulders, 2) tuck in the base of the abdomen and the buttocks, and 3) back to where we started, 'take a deep breath'.

CHAPTER THREE

Construction of the larynx

When the breath is expelled from the lungs by the action of the breathing apparatus, it passes first through the bronchial tubes, the BRONCHI. These are two short tubes, one branching from each lung, which enter into the base of the windpipe, the TRACHEA. This is another tube about four-and-a-half inches in length and one inch in diameter. Both bronchi and trachea are supplied with cartilaginous rings which prop them open and so prevent any kinking, which could cause a stoppage of the breath flow. (The structure of the trachea could be likened to that type of hosepipe in which metal rings are inserted for the purpose of ensuring a free flow of water.)

The top ring of the trachea is the summit of the air passage from the lungs, ie, the CRICOID CARTILAGE, and it is at this point that the breath enters into the organ of the voice, the LARYNX. This is a cavity formed by a framework of cartilages and joints, in which are positioned the VOCAL FOLDS. At the top of the windpipe, the trachea, are two membranous ligaments which arise from the walls of the larynx and form a narrow, slit-like opening, or fissure. They constitute the vocal folds. In female voices the vocal folds are approximately three-eights of an inch long and in male voices the length of the vocal folds is approximately half an inch. They lie horizontally across the larynx and in shape resemble an opening similar to that of a slender letter 'V'. The open stems of the 'V' are directed to the rear of the slit-like opening and are attached, one stem of each, to a pair of cartilages which are called the ARYTENOID CARTILAGES. The apex of the 'V' is directed to the front of the opening, where it is attached to another cartilage, called the THYROID CARTILAGE. The functions of these cartilages will be fully explained later in this chapter. The space between the stems of the 'V' is called THE CHINK OF THE GLOTTIS.

To complete the description of the larynx: lying above the vocal folds (which are known as the TRUE VOCAL FOLDS) are situated

CONSTRUCTION OF THE LARYNX

the FALSE VOCAL FOLDS, two loose folds of mucous membrane. They are positioned above the true vocal folds and protect them to a certain extent. They play no part in the production of vocal sound.

On either side of the larynx, in line with the true and false vocal folds and separating them, are the laryngeal pouches known as the FOLDS or VENTRICLES OF MORGAGNI. These are two small pouch-like cavities, placed at the rear of the false vocal folds. They contain glands which secrete a mucilaginous fluid that lubricates the vocal folds, keeping them in a moist condition.

The vocal folds are frequently referred to as vocal CORDS. This can be very misleading as it tends to give the impression that the voice is in some way a *stringed* instrument, which, of course, it is not. It will be seen that it more resembles an instrument of the reed family, for instance, an oboe. A correct definition of the vocal folds is given in a textbook of physiology as follows: 'Membranous folds or ligaments lying anteriorposteriorly across the larynx.'

The cavity of the larynx presents itself in the form of a triangular box. The base of the box is made by the CRICOID CARTILAGE, the top and the largest ring of the windpipe, the trachea. This cartilage, in shape, resembles a signet ring, the broad, deep portion formed by the seal or signet plate at the rear forming the back of the box, the narrow, more slender portion of the ring in front. It is immovable and forms the foundation of the larynx, to which other cartilages are attached.

The sides of the box are formed by the THYROID CARTILAGES. These are fashioned into two plates which form a two-sided shield, the two open ends of the plates directed to the back of the cricoid cartilage, the points of the plates being joined in the protuberance in front known as the 'Adam's Apple'. The thyroid cartilage is attached in a hinged fashion to either side of the cricoid cartilage, so that it is movable in a pivoting-like action.

On the uppermost part of the rim of the cricoid cartilage at the back, that portion which forms a seal or signet plate and which measures about one inch in height, are positioned a pair of cartilages called the ARYTENOID CARTILAGES. They are pyramidal in shape and are capable of two distinctly different movements. They can be rotated on their triangular bases in both inward and outward directions, and can also be moved in a forward and backward direction.

Above the box is what is sometimes called the lid cartilage, the

THE HUMAN VOICE AS A MUSICAL INSTRUMENT

EPIGLOTTIS. In shape it resembles a leaf and is situated between the base of the tongue and the upper opening of the larynx in an upright position. The top extremity is free and rounded like the broad part of a leaf; the lowest, stalk-like section has connections with the thyroid cartilage and the HYOID BONE which supports the tongue.

In the act of swallowing, the broad section of the epiglottis descends and covers the entrance to the larynx. This action directs the solids and liquids we consume into the gullet, the OESOPHAGUS, the muscular tube, about nine to ten inches long, that leads to the stomach. It also protects the larynx against accidental entry of foreign substances that might cause choking or coughing.

Before PHONATION − the onset of SOUND − in speech or singing is possible, certain adjustments in the *condition* and *approximation* of the vocal folds must take place. The word condition is used as a term for describing the tensions, length, and thickness of the edges of the ligaments. The ligaments alter in bulk as adjustments are made in pitch. Their magnitude is greater in the lower part of the vocal compass, in other words, one can say, thick. As the pitch of the voice is raised they become thinner. The term approximation is used to indicate the size and shape of the chink of the glottis. These actions bring about conditions which control the PITCH within the overall compass of the voice, as will be explained in detail in Chapter 4.

The adjustments are made by the movements of the cartilages of the larynx by their respective muscles which activate them. These actions can increase and relax the tensions of the vocal folds, lengthen them or shorten them and vary the amount of their approximations. This, combined with the correct functions of the breathing apparatus, controls the pitch of sound.

The breath drawn into or sent out from the lungs passes through the opening formed by the ligaments which constitute the vocal folds. In their reposed state for normal respiratory purposes, ie, silent inhalation and exhalation, there is little tension in the folds; they are fairly slack and fairly wide apart, so that no sound is produced as the breath passes between them. When vocal sound in speech or singing is required, the adjustments of the folds as directed above must take place so that they are brought into the correct condition and formation. As the breath impinges on them they are set into vibration and produce vocal sound.

The MUSCLES which control the movements and functions of the

CONSTRUCTION OF THE LARYNX

cartilages of the LARYNX to bring about the above-mentioned conditions of the vocal folds are as follows:

The muscles that control the TENSIONS, LENGTH and THICKNESS of the vocal folds are the CRICO-THYROID muscles, which, when contracted, move the thyroid cartilage in a downward and forward direction and so stretch the folds from the front of the glottis. An opposing pull to the rear of the glottis is made by the contraction of the POSTERIOR CRICO-ARYTENOID muscles. The RELAXATIONS of these tensions, lengths and thicknesses are brought about by the THYRO-ARYTENOID muscles, which work in opposition to the crico-thyroid muscles.

The APPROXIMATIONS of the vocal folds are made by the movement of the arytenoid cartilages, activated by the LATERAL CRICO-ARYTENOID muscles, which cause the arytenoid cartilages to rotate on their triangular bases in an inward direction, so bringing the folds closer together. The TRANSVERSE ARYTENOID muscle connects the two arytenoid cartilages to each other and assists in the drawing together of the vocal folds, which would now be positioned almost parallel to each other. In reverse to the closing of the chink of the glottis by the above actions, the widening of the space between the vocal folds at the chink of the glottis is made by the opposing action of the POSTERIOR CRICO-ARYTENOID muscles, which cause the rotation of the arytenoid cartilages in an outward direction.

CHAPTER FOUR

'Registers' and 'tessitura'

Registers

The various formations and condition of the vocal folds, brought about by the aforementioned actions, are termed REGISTERS. There are three overall formations made in the female voices, and two in the male voices. First and foremost, it must be born in mind that any changes in the various formations must at all times be made by a very gradual and controlled movement. The importance of the blending of the registers cannot be over-emphasized. (This particular aspect of vocal technique is fully discussed in Chapter 11.)

In the illustrations dealing with the compass of voices which follow it will be seen that the *gradual* approach from one register to another entails the movement of the voice through a series of notes that lie between the main register positions. These series are shown in small type between the main register divisions, which are also indicated.

The movement from one register to another must be anticipated before it actually takes place, so that the series overlap each other, thus blending the tonal quality and resonance of both together and ensuring that no breaks or sudden alterations are encountered in the vocal line.

In trained voices the ability to control the actions of the registers is made possible by the WILL. This is the faculty by which one decides what one shall do. Perhaps one may consider it the development of another 'sense' — that of a direction via the ear. We would PERCEIVE by the sense of hearing what is desired to take place. There is no other possible means whereby these changes in the conditions and formations of the vocal folds can take place. By the term registers one understands that the vocal folds undergo changes in their condition and formation. The folds alter in their tension and length, and the approximation and vibrating actions undergo changes to enable the different pitches in the overall compass of the voice to take place. Here follows a brief description of the state of the folds as they proceed through the registers.

As already stated, in the female voices there are three registers: these are given the terms LOW, MEDIUM and HIGH, or CHEST, MIDDLE and HEAD. In the low series of notes the folds will have sufficient tension to enable vibration which will take place over their whole length and thickness. As the voice moves up into the pitches of the higher series of notes in the middle range of the voice, the medium register, there will take place a change in the state of the folds but, again it must be stressed, in a very gradual and controlled fashion, so that the ear can detect no sudden alteration of tonal quality. At this point in the compass the folds will have become more tensed and thinner and there will be a closer approximation. The vibration will be taking place throughout their whole length, but on the inner edges of the folds only. As the voice continues into the highest series of pitches, there will be taking place another condition of the folds. Their tension will have increased, the approximation will now be greater, and the length of folds considerably shortened, leaving only about a third of their original length vibrating, again on the inner edges only. Combined with these formation changes, the ear will detect a blending of the tonal quality from the rather dark, sonorous quality of the lower part of the compass, to the more ringing, brighter quality of the top register. This, of course, one hears in all musical instruments. In some of those motivated by breath they are called by the same name, registers. Again, as already pointed out, it must be the aim of the singer to ensure that only imperceptable, gradual changes are allowed to take place, and this first over the whole of each series of notes, and then into the whole of three series, so that one senses one is using a single string and not as on stringed instruments of the present day. This controlled action is known as 'blending the registers' – a smooth transition from one to another. This aspect of technique will be fully discussed later.

The male voices consist of two registers which are termed the CHEST and MIXED registers. The actions, as applied to the female registers, take place in the same manner, but with a little difference in the condition of the folds, owing to their length being greater and the folds thicker. In the chest register the folds are quite tensed and vibrating in their whole length and thickness. They are well approximated and gradually both tension and approximation increase as the voice rises towards the beginning of the next series of notes, the mixed register. The gradual changes that so far have taken place continue and the folds now become more tensed and thinner in condition, and, in a slow controlled manner, the approximation is increased. The vibration is now taking place on the inner edges of the cords which have become thinner in condition. These two registers are more or less equally divided in the lower voices of the bass and baritone, and in the tenor voice, by a quarter and threequarters. The formation and conditions of the folds and their actions are similar.

Combined with the actions of the vocal folds in the registers of all voices, both male and female, changes must be made in the breath pressure and speed of the vibration of the folds, which are necessary to the overall accomplishment of good voice production and the control of pitch. Needless to mention, resonance plays a most important part in combination with the use of registers, and this aspect will be considered later.

The approximate range and series of notes that apply in the various registers of both male and female voices are as shown in the illustration opposite. There may be very slight difference as, naturally, all voices are very individual. The average compass required from all voice categories is approximately two octaves or a little more. However, certain cases have been recorded in which particular voices have covered a range of three octaves or even more, but these are, of course, extremely rare.

It will be observed that the coloratura soprano and the basso profundo voices are exceptional as far as compass is concerned. For instance, Astrofiammante (The Queen of the Night) in Mozart's *Die Zauberflöte*, is called upon for notes as high as F in alt many times. In *Der Rosenkavalier* the basso profundo, Baron Ochs, has to cover a range from the bottom C below the bass stave to G sharp above the stave.

In male voices, the low or chest register is used up to about

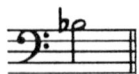

after which the mixed register, a combination of chest and head quality of tone, is used. The transition from one formation to another

'REGISTERS' AND 'TESSITURA'

in all voices must, of course, be very gradual, so that there is not even a suspicion of a sudden change but only a gliding feeling, as is the sound of the changing from one string to another on stringed instruments, made by the movement of the bow.

Tessitura

The word TESSITURA is used in connection with musical compositions to indicate the general pitch of notes in the overall compass of the instrument for which it is written. It stems from the Italian word *tessere*, meaning 'texture' or 'to weave'.

In vocal compositions the tessitura is determined by the particular voice for which it is intended, bearing in mind its natural tonal qualities.

Composers, being well aware of the generally accepted compasses and tonal qualities of the various voice categories, stay within those boundaries, using the medium register extensively. However, obviously for expressive and emotional reasons, and for climaxes of musical and verbal phrasing, they must occasionally use the extremes of the overall compass. Providing the singer's technique is absolutely under control, these demands can be met with security. But if the singer is called upon to *remain* for long periods in these extremities, either high or low, it is then correctly stated that the tessitura of the piece is very demanding. In the event of very high tessitura it could possibly impose strain on the voice and discomfort in the singing. In reverse, continual singing in the lower extremes could cause fatigue and weakness in the tone. If these conditions are experienced in the course of preparing a work, then the singer must give serious thought as to the suitability of the work for his or her particular voice. In the choice of songs there should be no problem; many of them are published in more than one key, and so it is only necessary to choose the most suitable one for the individual voice.

In connection with pitch, an example is very aptly stated by HC Deacon: 'The tessitura of vocal music in Beethoven's Ninth Symphony is justly the singer's nightmare.' Mahler's Eighth Symphony can also be mentioned in this respect. The tessitura for both chorus and soloist is extremely demanding, staying, as it does, for long periods in high extremes of pitch which can cause intonation difficulties and vocal discomfort.

CHAPTER FIVE

Resonation

A dictionary definition of RESONANT is 'resounding, echoing, continuation of sound'. Many ideas and suggestions have been expounded concerning voice resonation, and some have caused confusion. Terms such as 'chest voice', 'head voice', and so on, are inclined to give the impression that, by some means, vocal sound is produced from different places in the human instrument. However, it sometimes helps students to *imagine* such areas as points of the placement or resonance during early training and it does no harm. As we have seen in earlier references to the onset of sound, there is no possibility of the initial onset being produced anywhere other than at the chink of the glottis. It is there, and there only, that when the breath makes contact with the vibrating element, the vocal folds, sound is heard. This fundamental sound needs to be amplified and turned into full vocal tone by what is known as resonation. This is brought about by the fact that when the continuation of the sound is made possible by breath, it passes through various cavities in the human instrument. The main cavities of resonation are as follows:

The LARYNX, in which the vocal folds are situated. To a certain extent some resonation is set up there in view of the fact that it is constructed of a number of cartilages.

The PHARYNX is a most important resonator. It is a musculo-membranous tube situated behind the nose, mouth and the larynx. It is shaped somewhat like an inverted cone, so that the wide base is directed upwards, the apex downwards. It is about four-and-a-half inches in length, and it is broader in the transverse than in the antero-posterior diameter. The pharynx may be subdivided into three parts: (1) The nasal or naso-pharynx; that portion which lies behind the nostrils of the nose and above the soft palate. It is very important in the production of nasal *resonance* – not to be confused with nasal *tone* ('singing in the nose'), which is, of course, quite unacceptable. For this reason it always remains open, unlike the other two portions, which by muscular modification are capable of alterations in shape and expansion. (2) The oral pharynx, which reaches from the soft palate to the hyoid bone, from which the tongue rises. (3) The laryngeal pharynx is that portion of the cavity which reaches from the hyoid bone to the lower rim of the cricoid cartilage, where it is continuous with the oesophagus. To a considerable extent the pharynx is responsible for good tonal quality when accurately employed, and is sometimes referred to as the 'colouring resonator'.

The NASAL CAVITIES form the space at the back of the nose. This area of resonation is importantly linked with the brilliance of tone.

The SINUSES. They are hollow cavities in certain bones of the skull and face. Some connect with the nasal cavities and some with the temporal bone, which has a connection with the middle ear.

The MOUTH, the BUCCAL CAVITY, is another muscular cavity of the greatest importance. Together with the movements of the jaws, it can be altered in size and shape. It contains the TONGUE, which mainly forms the floor of the mouth. The HARD PALATE, which is immovable, forms the roof of the mouth and the floor of the nasal cavity. The hinder section of the hard palate joins with the fleshy SOFT PALATE, the VELUM, which is a membranous fold suspended from the border of the back part of the hard palate. It forms an incomplete partition between the mouth and the pharynx. From it hangs down a cone-shaped tag called the UVULA. On either side of the uvula are two folds of mucous membrane. These are called the PILLARS OF THE FAUCES, and they form the boundary of the opening from the mouth to the pharynx. This arch-like structure can easily be seen if one glances into a mirror so placed as to be able to see into the mouth, which should be shaped so as to produce the vowel ah. It is in this area that the pharynx, mouth and nose resonators meet with each other and combine to form a chamber of resonance.

Other cavities that play some part in resonation are those of the chest, the THORAX, the WINDPIPE, the TRACHEA, and the opening that leads from the larynx to the pharynx, the VESTIBULE OF THE PHARYNX. In the ordinary way the nasopharynx is the main entry for respiration via the mouth, but inhalation via the mouth is used by the singer for the reasons which have been stated.

Examples of resonation in some other musical instrument can be given. If one blows through the reed of, say, an oboe or bassoon, only a kind of 'squeak' will be produced. However, when the reed is placed in the instrument, the 'squeak' will be turned into the quality of sound associated with those instruments – a fine, full musical tone. This is brought about by the fact that now the 'squeak', the initial sound, or fundamental tone, is passed through the resonating cavities in the construction of the instrument. Likewise, if the string of the violin, viola, cello or any other members of the string family, played by a bow, is plucked with the fingers, only a very small staccato sound is produced. When the bow is applied to the string, however, the initial sound is amplified and given quality and, due to the resonation in the belly of the instrument, a continued smooth flow of tone results.

In conjunction with this are the effects brought about by what are known as 'harmonics' and 'overtones'. A brief, but sufficient explanation is as follows. A single note produced by a musical instrument can be called the fundamental note. This sets up the vibration of a number of attendant notes, and these colour and add quality to the tone by resonation. The actions in playing on instruments, other than the voice, can be felt and seen by the senses of touch and sight. The human instrument, however, is quite intangible and can only be played by the imagination and the will to perceive that we are directing vocal tone into the various spaces and cavities. We must always remember that the fundamental notes are produced at the glottis and resonated in the surrounding areas. The 'harmonics' and 'overtones' occur automatically when the singer has developed the voice with accurate technique. It will be observed that, eventually, a new 'sense' is born. One relies on this new sensation to bring about the correct placement of tone in the different registers of the voice.

As to the onset of sound in the voice, the examples of resonance used in connection with instruments of the wind family, and also of the string family, are, in a way, similar. By a short, staccato attack on the vocal folds, only a slight sound is heard. When the sound is continued on the breath, this initial 'squeak-like' sound is turned into a fuller vocal tone, which is then amplified and given quality and colour by its passing through the resonating cavities already mentioned. Some suggested means to experience the sensations of the placement of the tone are given in a later section.

It will be appreciated that it is felt necessary to include here a detailed description of the bones and cavities of the skull and face which play such an important part in resonation.

The lower jaw, the MANDIBLE, pivots from the TEMPORO-MANDIBULAR joint (between the temporal bone of the skull and the head of the mandible). This constitutes the lower part of the face.

The TEMPORAL BONE (one each side of the head, and which can be felt just behind and above the flat of the ear) is the skull bone through which the external auditory meatus passes. (MEATUS: a kind of canal or passage-way which is commonly called the 'ear-hole' to carry sounds into the middle ear after vibrating the TYMPANUM, or ear-drum.) Its fore-part forms, with the wing of the SPHENOID BONE, the 'temple'. (SPHENOID BONE: a wedge-shaped bone which articulates with the temporal bones.)

The NASAL BONES form the bridge of the nose. Behind them, and extending like blades cutting through on either side of the nasal septum (SEPTUM: a partition behind the two nasal cavities), are the plates of the ETHMOID BONES. (ETHMOID BONES: bones, together with their mucous membranes, which enter into the formation of the nose, are nasal resonators and they are affected when one has 'a cold in the nose'.)

CHAPTER SIX

Diction – the making of words and their enunciation

The term DICTION is sometimes applied to this aspect of singing. A better definition is ENUNCIATION, which embraces the correct articulatory actions in the production of consonants, and the moulding of vowels to produce fully comprehensible WORDS in both speech and singing.

The vocal instrument, the VOICE, is unique: it is the only one in the world that is able to express verbal and musical sounds simultaneously – the very essence of SONG – and singers must fully appreciate the tremendous advantage this gives over all other instruments as an added means of interpretation. The words must have an abundance of meaning by clarity in the articulation of consonants, and colourful vowels by their accurate moulding in the oral cavity, the mouth. The correct use of accentuation, stress, inflexion and punctuation in phrasing, which will ensure authentic, authoritative and convincing expression in presentation, is essential.

For such accomplished use of words it is emphasised that a good fundamental knowledge of the sister art to singing, that of elocution, should be the aim of all singers. The significance of perfection in word-making, enunciation, cannot be over-emphasised. If words are not felt to be completely concomitant and an adjunct to the singing voice, then deep consideration should be given as to the advisability of pursuing a career as a singer. There would be little use in the development of a good natural voice if, at the culmination of training, the words could not be understood.

As to the English language, one has heard it said that it is incompatible with singing. This is, of course, not the case, and one can only assume that it is mostly said by those who are not prepared to study it deeply enough to really learn of its beauty and how to convey it. It is a very expressive language and more than comparable with others thought by some to be 'more singable'.

THE HUMAN VOICE AS A MUSICAL INSTRUMENT

Making words

To understand how correct diction is accomplished it is necessary to have knowledge of the fundamentals of word-making. In the present case we are considering the English language.

Breath is the substance of speech. Having passed through the glottis, where it is transformed into voice, it enters the mouth (the oral cavity). The mouth is capable of assuming various shapes and sizes by the alteration of the condition and position of the tongue and the formation of the lips, together with the position of the jaw and the soft palate, both of which can be raised and lowered. The breath is moulded into VOWELS by these modifications in the aperture of the mouth from which it issues.

Vowels

These are the sounds heard when the breath flows uninterrupted through the mouth. The letters a, e, i, o, u are called vowels, as it is possible to sound them by themselves on a continuous stream of breath.

In the English language there are the following 13 simple vowel sounds:

a   as heard in ball, far, rate, mat
e   as heard in net, meet
i   as heard in rim
o   as heard in lot, folk
u   as heard in mute, full, fur, jut

Of these, i, as heard in pin, a, as heard in far, and u, as heard in full, are the primary vowels; all others are made by lengthening, combining or modifying these vowels.

For each sound produced there must be a specific formation of the mouth, together with the accurate positioning and condition of the organs of speech, namely the PHARYNX, the SOFT PALATE, the HARD PALATE, the TONGUE, the TEETH, the LIPS and the JAW. The CHEEKS also play their important part in the moulding of vowels. Their muscular actions are employed in the extension, retraction, narrowing and widening of the oral cavity.

The relationship between clear ENUNCIATION and good TONAL

QUALITY cannot be over-emphasized. The development of good voice production is dependent on the complete unification of these two elements – they cannot be divorced from each other. Distortion in vowel moulding and carelessness in articulation will result in poor tone and may even present difficulties with pitch, causing insecure intonation. One is often required to maintain vowel and tonal quality throughout a given period, i.e. in florid passages and runs to be sung on one vowel sound.

Classification of vowels

In the English language vowels have three classifications:

MONOPHTHONGS, which are divided into two types, termed LONG or SHORT;
DIPHTHONGS, which consist of two vowels (letters or sounds) pronounced as one syllable.
TRIPHTHONGS, which consist of a combination of three vowels (letters or sounds) which are made to form one sound.

1) MONOPHTHONGS (sometimes termed SIMPLE VOWELS) – These may be termed long or short. This terminology indicates their character and pronunciation in speech. For instance, in speech it is possible to prolong the duration of the vowel a in its long formation when pronouncing words such as far, laugh, marvellous, etc. It is not prolonged when used in its short formation, for instance in words like fat, chatter, matter, etc. However, in singing, all monophthongs, long or short, can be sustained for any specified duration, as they must be, when a word is continued in florid movements or running passages.

2) DIPHTHONGS (sometimes termed COMPOUND VOWELS) – These consist of a sequence of two distinct vowels, letters or sounds which are smoothly linked together to sound as only one syllable. For example, by linking the vowel $\bar{a}r$ as heard in the word mare, and the vowel $\bar{i}$ as heard in the word bit, the diphthong vowel sound is heard in word such as lay, prey, gauge, phrase, and so on. There is a rule to be observed in the pronunciation of diphthongs. The first element is emphasised and sustained, the second is treated in a very light, short manner, making it almost indiscernible. Never must both elements have the same duration. However, it must be observed that

an exception to the rule occurs when the diphthong vowel sound ū is employed in words such as due, youth, beauty, few, view, etc. which are produced by the linking together of the vowels ē and ōō. Here the first element is made very short, brief and hardly discernible, so that the stress falls on the second element which bears the emphasis in pronunciation.

3) TRIPHTHONGS (sometimes also termed COMPOUND vowels) – These consist of the union of three distinct vowels, letters or sounds which, when sounding in pronunciation, must be heard as only one syllable. The vowel ā when constituting a triphthong in words like layer, conveyor, greyer, etc. is made up of the three vowels, ār as heard in a word like mare, ē as heard in a word like eat, and the hardly discernible vowel e or er. The stress in triphthongs is put on the first element, the second and third elements being treated in a very ineffectual manner, hardly discernible.

The above rule governing the manner of the use of compound vowels must be strictly observed at all times. This is especially necessary in singing where, in the execution of runs often entailing a long series of notes to be sung on a word made by a diphthong or triphthong, or in a florid passage making the same demands, it is essential that the first element of the vowel bearing the stress in pronunciation is continuous for the specified duration. It must not be changed into the second or the second and third elements of the vowel. It is also essential that no change in the quality of the stressed element takes place in the negotiation of changes of pitch encountered in such passages, which would result in the distortion of the vowel. Also, in using compound vowels the transition from one vowel to another must never be sudden or disconnected, but always in a smooth and gliding manner. Suggestions will be made later in relation to VOWEL GLIDES to help develop this ability which will enhance development of good enunciation.

Lastly, attention must be drawn to the NEUTRAL e – this is the most common sound in the English language and is used only in unaccented positions in words. It is heard in many spelling forms. Some examples are: *the* book, account, murmur, gentleman, etc.

Consonants

Consonants are produced by the use of the organs of articulation. They include the PHARYNX, that part of the throat which lies behind the soft palate; the SOFT PALATE itself; the HARD PALATE; the TONGUE; the TEETH; the LIPS; the JAW; and the CHEEKS. These organs are divided into two groups, one group being termed ACTIVE, the others PASSIVE.

Those which are classified as active are the SOFT PALATE, the TONGUE, the LOWER JAW and the LOWER LIP. Those termed passive are the HARD PALATE, the UPPER GUM and the TEETH. The tongue works with great mobility from and to the ridge of the UPPER GUM – commonly termed the ALVEOLAR. (The roots of the teeth are firmly embedded in the ridges of the upper and lower gums. These ridges are called the ALVEOLI. To some extent the UPPER LIP can be judged as active, but is perhaps more justly termed as passive in view of the actions made against it by the lower lip. Also a certain amount of movement of the cheeks take place.

The actions of the articulatory organs can either partially interrupt the issue of breath or, on occasion, can cause a momentary complete stoppage of the air stream. However, there are exceptions where no interruption of the air stream takes place at all. The three divisions are termed FULLY VOICED, PARTIALLY VOICED or UNVOICED consonants. A full explanation of them will be given later.

Classification of consonants

Consonants can be classified by the various actions which take place in their production. The descriptions of these actions are as follows:

1) LABIALS (with the lips) – By the upward movement of the jaw, the lower and top lips are brought into contact with each other, so completely closing the aperture of the mouth. This is the necessary action to produce such consonants as b, p and m in words such as beat, bone, pear, peat, meat, and most.

2) LABIO-DENTALS (with the lips and teeth) – By placing the top teeth to make contact with the lower lip, the consonants v and f are produced, heard in words such as vain, vocal, love, brave and fine, fresh, turf, trifle, etc.

3) LINGUA-DENTALS (with the tongue and the teeth) — The tongue is an extremely mobile organ, being supplied with two groups of muscles, some of which are in the tongue itself and others the terminal fibres of which pass into the mouth, primarily the lower jaw. The first group accounts for its ability to change its condition, ie, contraction, relaxation, shape, etc. The second group is responsible for the various functions of extension, retraction, elevation and depression. In words employing the consonants d and t, the front portion of the tongue touches the ridge of the top front teeth, the middle portion making contact with the central top teeth to produce such words as down, sad, touch, fate, etc.

4) LINGUA-PALATAL (with the tongue and either the hard or soft palate) — The hard palate forms the roof of the mouth and the floor of the nasal cavity. It extends from the ridge of the top teeth, in which their roots are situated, to the soft palate, the area at the back of the mouth, where the uvula may be seen to be hanging down from its arch-like structure. In forming such consonants as l, or the rolled r, the tip of the tongue is, in the first instance, brought into contact with the alveolar ridge and will be used to produce such words as love, stroll, gently, etc. In the second instance, when it occurs in words such as rage, rushing, rolling, etc, the tip of the tongue is raised to trill a little further back on the hard palate. The root of the tongue and the soft palate are also used in the articulation of some lingua-palatal consonants. For instance, where g or k is used in such words as good, king, tug, take, etc, the back portion of the tongue is raised to make contact with the lowered soft palate, so producing the guttural sound which is perceptible in words where they are used.

DEFINITION OF VOICED, PARTIALLY VOICED AND UN-VOICED CONSONANTS — The terms voiced, partially voiced or unvoiced, applied to consonants, indicate those in which a full or partial vibration of the vocal folds takes place in their production, or where no vibration whatsoever is made. For instance, in words where the consonant l occurs as in love, pull, etc, m as in more, roam etc, n as in no, lone, etc, ng as in song, among, etc, in each case these consonants can be continous, and are termed VOICED consonants. On such fully voiced consonants it is possible to sound any passage of music, at all pitches, as long as the breath-flow continues. In the case of the consonants b as in book, lobe, etc, d as in dole, road, etc, v as in voice, thrive, and so on, a very slight vibration of the vocal folds is experienced in a guttural sound. Such consonants are termed PARTIALLY VOICED. Where no vibration of the folds takes place in producing p, t, f, etc, in such words as pity, took, pine, the consonants so used are termed UNVOICED.

ALLIED or PAIRED CONSONANTS – Some consonants are formed by identical actions of articulatory organs. For instance, p and b; t and d; f and v. Such a pair of consonants are termed ALLIED consonants.

Now follows an ALPHABET CHART which gives full details of the manner in which vowels are formed and consonants articulated by the positioning and actions of the speech organs which are employed in word-making.

THE HUMAN VOICE AS A MUSICAL INSTRUMENT

ALPHABET CHART

The following chart describes the movements of the active articulatory organs of speech to produce CONSONANTS and the correct manner in which the oral cavity, the mouth, is moulded and modified to produce the various VOWELS which makes possible correct and fully comprehensible WORDS. It is intended to be used as a guide in ensuring the correct combination in the use of consonants and vowels and to help correct faults that may arise which could seriously affect good enunciation and tonal quality.

The phonetic symbols which appear in the chart are used to indicate the quality or character of the vowels used in pronunciation of the word. For instance, in words such as see, theme, seat, etc, the symbol ¯ is placed above the vowel to indicate the sound as being that of the long monophthong vowel ē. In indicating the pronunciation of the vowel in words such as met, tense, when, the symbol ˘ is placed above, thus: ĕ. When a vowel is to be heard in its diphthongal sound, for instance the vowel i, as used in words such as sign, night, white, mite, etc, the symbol ¯ is placed above it, Ī. When it is to be heard in its short monophthong form in words such as fit, write, chit, etc, the symbol ˘ is used, ĭ. When it appears merely as i, it indicates that it is barely audible, as in words such as basin, cousin, etc. It is pointed out that all words given as examples, no matter what form of spelling is used, are to be heard by their phonetic sounds as indicated by symbols.

A – Short monophthong vowel ă, as heard in words such as fat, chat, matter, etc. In forming this vowel the mouth is approximately half open, the middle part of the tongue is slightly arched by retraction into an almost smiling position but in no way must this be exaggerated into a grin. The breath flows freely through a spacious aperture in the mouth.

A – Short monophthong vowel heard in words like watch, waft, want, waffle, etc. This sound, phonetically the same as the vowel ŏ as in got, is executed by the narrowing of the mouth by the contraction of muscles of the cheeks and protruding the lips to form a circular aperture for the issue of the vowel. The tongue is slightly retracted in the spacious oral cavity.

A – Short monophthong vowel âr, heard in words such as many, fare, anything. This sound, phonetically the same as the vowel ĕ as in get, is produced with

DICTION

the jaw dropped and the tongue slightly arched to make contact with the inside edges of the middle top teeth. The breath flows through a spacious mouth.

A – Long monophthong vowel sounding in words like raw, ball, maud, crawl, etc. This vowel sound, phonetically the same as oor as in more, is formed by the narrowing of the oral channel by drawing in the cheeks and extending the lips to form a firm circular aperture for the issue of the word to be made. The breath flows through the somewhat reduced space in the mouth.

A – The almost indiscernible vowel a when occuring in words such as account, tradesman, banana, etc. It is treated in a manner similar to that of the neutral e or er sound. (The neutral e is fully described under the alphabet E later in this chart.)

A – Long monophthong vowel ar as heard in words such as far, palm, charm, laugh, etc. In forming this vowel, the mouth is in its freest state – there is no contraction made in the oral cavity; it is relaxed into a large aperture through which the breath issues unobstructed. The word Ah is used in expressing many different emotions, such as delight, disgust, sorrow, joy, admiration, etc. Because of the freedom in its production it is used extensively in exercises in the study of voice production, especially in singing. It is considered to be the first sound heard from infants, being so simple in formation.

A – The diphthong vowel ā heard in words such as day, grey, lane, great, freight, etc. It consists of the two distinct vowels, those of approximately the ar heard in the word fare and ĭ as heard in fit. They must be linked together so as to sound as only one syllable, laying a stress on the first element of the diphthong. In forming this sound the first element is made with the jaw hanging down loosely and the tongue relaxed and lying flat in the mouth. The breath flows freely through a large aperture. To bring about the second element there is a rapid upward movement of the jaw, and the tongue rises to an arched position in the mouth, its middle outside edges making contact with the inside edges of the middle top teeth to form, and to very quickly terminate, the sound, with the hardly discernible vowel i.

A – The triphthong vowel heard in words such as layer, gayer, greyer, betrayer, conveyor, etc. This sound is made by a sequence of three distinct vowels, linked together to sound as only one syllable, those of approximately ar as heard in the word fare, the voewl ē, and the hardly discernible neutral e or er vowel. The first of the three elements which constitute this triphthong, the ar, which bears the stress in pronunciation, is made with the jaw dropped loosely to enable a fairly open mouth in which the tongue lies flattened, so forming a spacious oral cavity for its issue. To bring about the formation of the mouth

THE HUMAN VOICE AS A MUSICAL INSTRUMENT

for the second and third elements, there is a rapid upward movement of the jaw and the tongue rises into an arched position in the mouth, making a contact with the inside edges of the middle top teeth to form the neutral e or er vowel for the termination of the triphthong.

B – Partially voiced labial consonant heard in words such as bar, barb, rub, trouble, bubble, etc. It is formed by firmly pressing together the lips, so causing a complete closure of the mouth and stopping the flow of breath. As the air is sent into the closed mouth an audible, muffled, humming-like sound is heard momentarily before the parting of the lips to allow the issue of the breath to be moulded into vowels or articulated into consonants. This consonant is sometimes placed in the category called implosive which also includes consonants D, G, K.

C – When heard in its hard character, occurring before the vowels a, o and u, and some consonants, it is sounded as K, and classified as an unvoiced lingua-palatal implosive or stop consonant. It is heard in such words as calm, chaos, clinic, tobacco, specific, traffic, etc. For its production the jaw is approximately half raised and the root of the tongue is raised to make contact with the soft palate. This action causes the obstruction of the breath flow by a glottal stop. On the release of this obstruction by dropping the jaw and lowering the tongue, a momentary muffled guttural sound is heard as the air is allowed to flow freely for the utterance of consonants or vowels for the making of the word.

C – When heard in its soft character as an unvoiced sibilant, also termed fricative consonant. When occuring before e, i and y in such words as centre, civilian, cycle, it is sounded as the consonant S and produced in the same articulatory manner. It is formed with the jaw raised and the tip of the tongue placed firmly against the ridge of the top front teeth and arched in its middle part, making contact with the hard palate. As the breath is sent out it passes through the very narrow aperture between the teeth ridge, the alveolar and the tip of the tongue in a hissing sound. The contact of the tongue and the alveolar ridge is released and the middle part of the tongue flattened to allow a free passage of the breath for the production of a vowel or consonant.

CH – When heard in its hard character as an unvoiced lingua-palatal implosive or stop consonant, sounded as the consonant K, and formed in the same manner when occuring before the vowel a, o and u, and some consonants, it is heard in such words as chaos, choral, chord, character, etc. For its formation the jaw is raised, approximately half way, and the root of the tongue is raised to make contact with the soft palate, so causing the obstruction of the air-flow by a glottal stop. On the release of this obstruction by the lowering of the jaw and descending of the tongue, a momentary guttural sound is heard as the air is allowed to flow freely for the utterance of consonants or vowels.

DICTION

CH — In its soft character as an unvoiced palatal affricate consonant, as sounding in words such as cheer, chip, charm, pinch, touch, etc. It is produced by placing the tip of the tongue firmly against the aveolar ridge with the jaw raised, so causing a momentary stoppage in the flow of breath. As the contact of the tongue and alveolar is relinquished, the escape of air is heard to enable the articulation of words.

D — Partially voiced lingua-palatal consonant, heard in words such as do, drop, tend, dental, etc. In its formation the jaw is raised so that the lower and top teeth are in close proximity and the front portion of the tongue is placed firmly against the alveolar ridge. As the breath is set in motion a slight gluttural sound is heard before the articulatory position is disengaged to allow its issue for the consonant or vowel to be used in the making of the word to follow. (D and T are allied consonants as both are produced in the same articulatory manner.)

E — Short monophthong vowel ĕ heard in words such as pet, debt, gentle, general, etc. In forming this sound the middle section of the tongue is felt to be making contact with the inside edges of the middle top teeth with only just a slight pressure. The breath flows freely through quite a spacious aperture in the mouth.

E — Long monophthong vowel ē heard in words like weep, cheap, lean, etc. In forming this sound the jaw is raised and the middle part of the tongue is arched enough to make a light contact with the inside edges of the middle top teeth, the corners of the mouth tending towards a smiling position which, however, must in no way be exaggerated into a grin. The tip of the tongue is quite free and the breath flows freely through a spacious aperture.

E — The neutral e sound. This is the most common sound in the English language, heard in many different ways of spelling but only used in unaccented positions in words. For instance, pure, tour, ago, sailor, and so on.

ER — Short monophthong vowel ēr sounding in words such as term, firm, churn, learn, earnest, early, etc. In forming this sound there is not a great deal of space between the top and lower teeth. The jaw is dropped a little, the tongue is flat and quite relaxed. The breath issues through a spacious mouth. This vowel is sometimes treated in a neutral manner; for instance in words like maker, later, etc.

E — Diphthong vowel consisting of the long vowel ē as heard in such words as weep, cheap, etc, linked with scarcely audible neutral er to sound as only one syllable in words such as fear, bier, steer, etc. To form the first element

THE HUMAN VOICE AS A MUSICAL INSTRUMENT

of the sound, the jaw is raised and the edges of the middle part of the tongue make contact with the inside edges of the middle top teeth. The air flows through a somewhat restricted oral cavity. To terminate the diphthong on the hardly discernible neutral er, the jaw is dropped and the contact of the tongue and teeth is released.

E – Diphthong vowel, consisting of the short vowel ĕ as heard in such words as met, get, ware, chair, etc. linked to the hardly discernible er vowel and made to sound as only one syllable in words like heir, pair, where'er, etc. This is formed with the jaw lowered for the first element so that the air flows freely through a fairly spacious oral cavity, the middle edges of the tongue making contact with the inside edges of the middle top teeth. To bring about the second element of the diphthong, the jaw is slightly raised and the contact of the tongue and teeth released.

F – Unvoiced labio-dental fricative consonant heard in such words as fine, fling, fluff, truffle, tough, etc. It is formed by placing the top front teeth on the lower lip, when the air will be heard to issue through the narrow opening so moulded, with no voiced sound. In the relinquishment of the contact of the teeth and the lip by dropping the jaw, the breath is allowed to flow freely for the articulation of words. The same sound of the consonant F is heard, and made, by a similar articulatory action, in words where PH occurs, such as physic, phail, graph, telephonic, etc. (F and V are allied consonants, both being formed by the same articulatory action.)

G – Partially voiced lingua-palatal implosive or stop consonant when used in its hard form in such words as go, game, guard, tag, regard, begone, etc. In its production the jaw is raised and the root of the tongue makes contact with the soft palate, being arched in the back of the mouth, so causing an obstruction of the air stream by a glottal stop. On the release of this obstruction by dropping the jaw and lowering the tongue, a momentary guttural sound is heard as the air is allowed to issue freely for the utterance of consonants and vowels in the making of words.

G – In its soft form as partially voiced lingua-palatal affricate consonant, heard in words such as gem, gentle, ginger, rigid, rage, ridge, etc. It is formed with the jaw raised and the front part of the tongue pressed quite firmly against the alveolar ridge, the middle section being arched to make contact with the hard palate. This causes a momentary stoppage of the breath before the onset of the vowel or consonant, when a slight guttural stop will be heard. On the release of the contact of the tongue and hard palate, the breath issues freely for the enunciation of the vowel or consonant of the word to be made. The contact of tongue and palate takes place momentarily in the same articulatory action in the middle and endings of words.

DICTION

H – Unvoiced aspirate consonant. In its production the mouth is completely open and only the emission of breath takes place, as when breathing on a mirror or warming the hands, sighing, etc. The jaw is dropped and the tongue lies flat in the mouth and both move for the subsequent formation of vowels.

I – Short monophthong vowel ĭ heard in words like it, bit, jig, trip, glitter, etc. It is produced by the jaw being raised and the edges of the central part of the arched tongue making contact with the inside edges of the middle top teeth. The oral channel is free so that air can flow through it quite easily.

I – The vowel i when occuring in words such as basin, cousin, etc, is treated in a neutral manner, being hardly discernible.

I – Diphthong vowel Ī consists of a sequence of two distinct vowels, that of approximately the vowel ah when sounded in a word like path (it should be noted that there is a slight difference in the character of this sound and that of the long monophthong ār when sounding in a word such as far) and the vowel i as heard in words such as fit, kit etc. The two vowels must be linked together in a smooth manner and sounded as only one syllable. In forming this sound, heard in words such as fly, time, high, height, guidance, etc, the air issues through a completely open mouth on the first element of the diphthong which is stressed. For the second element a rapid upward movement of the jaw takes place. The tongue which has been lying quite flat in the mouth also rises rapidly so that its middle edges make contact with the inside edges of the middle top teeth to produce the almost indiscernible vowel i to terminate the diphthong.

I – Triphthong vowel heard in such words as fire, liar, shire, science, etc. It consists of three distinct vowels which are linked together to sound as only syllable. They are the vowels of approximately ah as heard in a word like path, the vowel ē as heard in a word like meet, and the neutral e or er vowel. In forming this sound, the first element of the triphthong is made by shaping the vowel ah. Here the jaw is dropped and the tongue lies flat in the mouth. The air flows freely through the large oral cavity. To terminate the triphthong, a rapid upward movement of the jaw and tongue takes place. The tongue in this movement rises so that its middle edges come into contact with the inside edges of the middle top teeth to form the second element, the vowel e. Both the jaw and the tongue then quickly relax into a neutral, barely discernible e or er to terminate the triphthong.

J – Partially voiced lingua-palatal affricate consonant heard in such words as jaw, joint, adjust, rejoice, etc. In its production the front part of the tongue is placed firmly against the alveolar ridge, with the middle section raised to

THE HUMAN VOICE AS A MUSICAL INSTRUMENT

make contact with the hard palate. The flow of the breath is stopped by this formation. By dropping the jaw and releasing the contact of the tongue and the palate, the passage of breath is freed to enable the moulding of vowels in the mouth. As it issues for this purpose a slight friction is heard to take place.

K – Unvoiced lingua-palatal implosive or stop consonant heard in words such as kite, take, kiosk, forsaken, etc. In making this consonant the root of the tongue is raised to make contact with lowered soft palate, so causing stoppage of the air-flow. As the contact of the tongue and palate is relinquished by dropping the jaw and tongue and raising the soft palate, a slight guttural sound is heard to take place, immediately followed by the flow of breath to allow the articulation of a consonant or moulding of a vowel for the word to be made. In words when the initial consonant K is followed by the consonant N, ie, in know, knack, knight, etc, the K is not sounded. Such words commence with the sound of N.

L – Voiced lingua-palatal consonant, sometimes known as a liquid or semi-vowel. This is due to the fact that its sound can be maintained for any specified duration. It is formed by placing the front part of the tongue against the very front part of the hard palate where it meets the alveolar, with the mouth in a fairly open condition, and sending out the breath which issues freely. It is heard in words like love, longing, full, tool, total, etc. When occuring in the middle of words such as calm, folk, should, it is not sounded.

M – Voiced labial consonant made by the compression of the lips. It is sometimes termed a liquid consonant due to the fact that its sound can be maintained for any specified duration. It is mostly nasal in resonance, as the sound passes gently through the nostrils in a humming manner in words such as moon, roaming, gloomy, murmur, etc. The lips are parted and the breath issues via the mouth for the formation of the vowel in the word to be produced.

N – Voiced lingua-palatal consonant. This is termed a liquid consonant as it can be sounded for any specified duration in speech and singing. It is heard in words such as now, nave, groan, nonsense, luncheon, tune, etc. It is formed by placing the tip of the tongue firmly against the curve of the hard palate where it meets the alveolar ridge. It is nasal in quality as the breath issues through the nostrils in a continuous humming sound. The lips are not compressed but are left well parted. By a further lowering of the jaw and tongue, the contact of the tongue and palate is released and the breath flows freely through the mouth to mould the vowel to be used in making words.

(The voiced consonants L, M, and N are used to a great extent in exercises for the development of certain aspects of singing techniques. By using them to preceed vowel sounds, the placing and onset of phonation of notes or phrases in various pitches and their resonating areas are more easily sensed and experienced in practise.)

DICTION

NG — Voiced lingua-palatal consonant heard in words like song, string, strong, hung, etc. It is termed a liquid consonant or semi-vowel as its nasal sound can be maintained for any specified duration. It is formed by the root of the tongue being raised to make a contact with the lowered soft-palate, so stopping the emission of breath via the mouth and directing its issue through the nostrils in a continuous humming sound. When, by lowering the tongue and raising the soft palate, their contact is released the breath flow can be transferred to the mouth to enable the production of consonant or vowels for making words.

O — Short monophthong vowel ŏ heard in such words as not, gone, yacht, dollar, quality, etc. It is formed with the mouth, giving a large aperture for the issue of the breath. The tip of the tongue lightly touches the ridge of the lower front teeth.

O — Diphthong vowel ō consisting of two distinct vowels: approximately the vowel ŭ, as heard in a word such as surge, and the vowel o͞o which, when smoothly linked together, produce the sound heard in words like oh, most, though, brogue, oak, etc. The two vowels must be heard as one syllable; the first element of the diphthong bears the stress, the second is treated in a very ineffectual manner, being hardly discernible. In forming this sound the tongue is in a fairly firm condition and the mouth is slightly protracted for the first element, through which the air flows freely in the quite spacious cavity. To terminate the diphthong there is a rapid further protraction of the mouth so that the lips are made to form into a small circular aperture for the second element, the o͞o which is made hardly discernible. (This vowel is regarded by some as a monophthong and not as a diphthong at all. However by acute and careful listening to its use in such words as given above, it will reveal that the vowel o͞o is present, but that it is, as pointed out, hardly discernible. In the opinion of the writer, it should be designated as a diphthong.) The word oh produces the exclamation of many emotions of sorrow, desire, pain, fear, delight, etc, and can be regarded as important as ah for this purpose.

O — In some instances the vowel o is treated in a neutral fashion; for example, in words like wagon, flagon, dragon, where it plays no effective part, being hardly discernible.

OI — Diphthong vowel, heard in such words as boil, boy, join, moist, oyster, etc. It consists of a sequence of the two vowels, ôr and i, linked smoothly together to form only one syllable. The breath flows freely through the spacious formation of the first element of the diphthong, the mouth being protracted to shape a good opening at the lips for the vowel ôr. This is followed by a rapid retraction of the corners of the mouth, together with a slight retraction and raising of the tongue, to complete the second element, i, which is made very short and almost indiscernible.

THE HUMAN VOICE AS A MUSICAL INSTRUMENT

OO – Long monophthong vowel o̅o̅. In forming this vowel, which is heard in words like moon, construe, crew, lose, etc, the mouth is well protracted, the lips forming a small circular aperture for the issue of this sound. The tongue is firm in condition and slightly retracted in the mouth. The breath flows freely through a somewhat narrowed oral cavity.

OO – Short monophthong vowel ŏŏ. It is formed by the protrusion of the front of the mouth by drawing in the cheeks, so narrowing the oral channel to some extent. The lips are formed into a circular aperture for the issue of this vowel, heard in words such as hook, look, would, forsook, etc. The breath flows freely through the somewhat reduced cavity in the mouth.

OR – Long monophthong vowel ôr heard in words such as fort, taught, short, report, etc. It is formed with the cheeks drawn in slightly, the lips protracted to form a fairly large aperture for the issue of this sound and the tongue retracted but not raised or stiffened in any way. The breath flows easily through quite a spacious oral cavity.

OW – Diphthong vowel ow, heard in words such as brow, cloud, plough, howling, etc. It consists of two distinct vowels, that of approximately the vowel ah, as heard in such words as rather or mark, and the vowel o̅o̅, which, when they are linked together, constitute only one syllable. For the issue of the first element of the diphthong the oral cavity is shaped in its freest state, the mouth well opened and the tongue lying flat therein. To bring about the second element, which must be made very short and hardly discernible, there is a rapid upward movement of the jaw and the mouth is protracted by drawing in the cheeks, so narrowing the oral channel, to form a small circular opening with the lips, for the issue of the vowel o̅o̅ to terminate the diphthong. The breath flows freely on the first element, which, on occasion, may have to be maintained in singing a series of notes in runs or florid movements in the music.

OWR – Triphthong vowel owr. This consists of a sequence of three distinct vowels, those of the approximate ah, as heard in a word like father, the vowel o̅o̅ and the neutral vowel e or er. They must be linked together so as to sound as one syllable, such as in words like power, devour, allowance, etc. This sound is formed with the jaw hanging loosely so that the mouth is well opened, with the tongue lying flat therein for the first element of the triphthong, the ah. This first element bears the stress for the required duration in speech and in singing. To bring about the second element, a rapid upward movement of the jaw is made, together with the protraction of the lips by drawing in the cheeks to shape the vowel o̅o̅. This is equally rapidly followed by the complete relaxation of the shape to terminate the third element of the triphthong, the hardly discernible neutral e or er.

DICTION

P — Unvoiced labial, implosive or stop consonant, heard in words such as pay, paint, plumb, trap, tip, etc. In forming this consonant the lips are pressed firmly together, causing a complete stoppage of the air. On parting the contact of the lips a slight gentle emission of the breath is heard before the articulation of a consonant or moulding of a vowel takes place for word-making. (P is allied to B as both are made by the same articulatory action.)

Q — This consonant can be formed and heard in two different manners:

1) A combination of the unvoiced implosive or stop consonant, K, and the semi-vowel, W, closely linked together so as to produce only the single sound heard in words like quick, queen, quota, quantity, etc. It is formed with the jaw raised and the root of the tongue making contact with the soft palate, as in forming the consonant K, so causing the stoppage of the breath. A very rapid movement follows immediately, made by dropping the jaw, thus releasing the contact of the tongue and the soft palate, to sound the semi-vowel W (pronounced phonetically oo-er) which issues with a slight sound of the freed air, to enable the enunciation of the word to be made.

2) In very few cases, as an implosive or stop consonant, heard merely as K and formed in the same manner as that consonant (please see above). It is heard in the words quay, queue, quoit.

R — Voiced lingua-palatal fricative consonant, distinctly pronounced in its rolled form only when it begins a word or syllable, for instance, in words like raw, rage, round. The rolled R can be continued for any specified duration. It is made by the expiration of the breath whilst the tip of the tongue touches the roof of the mouth with a quick tremulous motion, during which there is a free passage of air through a spacious oral cavity. The pronunciation of this letter of the alphabet is considered to be more difficult than any other letter in the alphabet of the English language. It is the last to be learnt by children, and even some adults find its execution difficult and at times impossible if the tongue is too thick, or is too closely connected to the lower part of the mouth. However, it is necessary for correct English speech and essential for singers, where it must be clearly heard. It is a sound very distinctive in both the Italian and German languages and plays an intrinsic part in the accurate articulation and pronunciation of words in those languages which are so much in demand from singers. After most vowels the consonant R is heard only as an impediment of the emission of the breath, when the tip of the tongue is brought near to the roof of the mouth but does not actually touch it. For example, after the vowel a in words such as bar, farther, etc, or the vowel o, as in tor, torn, corner, etc, the R is scarcely heard at all.

THE HUMAN VOICE AS A MUSICAL INSTRUMENT

S — Unvoiced lingua-dental fricative consonant heard in words like so, suffer, soup, pass, paste, etc. It is produced by placing the tip of the tongue behind the lower teeth, followed by the sending out of the breath during which a hissing sound is heard as the air issues through the small aperture so formed. This consonant is also termed sibilant. (S and Z are allied consonants, both being formed with the same articulatory action, the only difference being the hissing sound in S and the partially voiced buzzing sound produced by Z.)

T — Unvoiced lingua-palatal implosive or stop consonant, in words such as top, tent, tender, content, pointing, etc. In forming this consonant the jaw is raised, and the tip of the tongue is placed firmly against the ridge of the top front teeth, the alveolar, so causing a stoppage in the flow of breath. For the production of a word or syllable this contact is relinquished by dropping the jaw and the tongue, to allow a free issue of breath to articulate a consonant or form a vowel. As the contact is released, a slight explosive sound made by the emission of the breath is heard to take place. (T and D are allied consonants as both are produced with the same articulatory action.)

TH — Partially voiced lingua-dental fricative consonant, heard in words such as thou, then, therefore, though, etc. For the production of this consonant, the jaw is raised, the front part of the tongue is placed firmly against the ridge of the top teeth, the alveolar. When breath is sent into the mouth a slight guttural sound is heard to take place, after which the breath flow is stopped. To make possible the formation of vowels following this consonant, the contact of the tongue and the teeth is relinquished by dropping the jaw and lowering the tongue, so enabling the necessary free emission of the breath. (It is considered by some that this consonant consists more of DH than TH. No doubt this is due to the guttural sound heard in its onset.)

TH — Unvoiced lingua-dental fricative consonant heard in words such as think, thigh, thank, thatch, thimble, etc. For its formation, the jaw is raised and the tip of the tongue is placed lightly on the top middle teeth. As the air is sent out, a slight friction is heard as it emerges through the small aperture that has been formed. The contact of the tongue and the teeth is released by dropping the jaw and lowering the tongue, so allowing a free flow of breath through a spacious cavity for the moulding of vowels for the words to be made.

U — Short monophthong vowel ŭ heard in words such as upon, undo, dug, supper, trudge, etc. In forming this vowel, the mouth is well opened, the tongue is slightly raised and retracted, its tip being quite free. The corners of the mouth are a little retracted towards a smile, but must in no way be exaggerated into a grin.

DICTION

U — When appearing in words such as bonus, sinus, census, etc, this consonant is treated in a very neutral, ineffectual manner, being hardly discernible.

U — Short monophthong as heard in such words as put, full, bull, etc. It is formed in the same manner as the vowel o͝o in words like book, shook, etc.

U — Long monophthong as heard in such words as true, glue, flute, etc. It is formed in the same manner as the vowel ō͞o in words like loot, shoot, gloomy.

U — Diphthong vowel u consisting of two distinct vowels, ē and ō͞o, which are linked together to sound as only one syllable. Heard in words such as you, due, view, unit, useful, etc. In producing this sound the jaw is raised and so is the tongue, the middle edges of which make contact with the inside edges of the middle top teeth to produce the first element of the diphthong, the ē. The second element, the ō͞o, is produced by a rapid protraction of the mouth and the lips to form the circular aperture for the issue of this vowel, which flows freely on the breath. It must be noted that this particular vowel differs greatly from other diphthongs in that the first element is not prolonged but made very short, hardly discernible, so that the stress in pronunciation is laid entirely on the second element.

UR — Diphthong vowel, made by the two vowels, ō͞o and the neutral e or er, which are linked together to sound as only one syllable, heard in words such as dour, tour, adjure, etc. It is produced by the protraction of the lips and narrowing of the mouth to form a small circular aperture for the issue of the first element of the diphthong, the ō͞o, which bears the stress in pronunciation. This is followed by a rapid drop of the jaw and retraction of the lips into quite a large cavity in the mouth for the barely discernible second element, the neutral e or er to terminate the diphthong.

V — Partially voiced labio-dental fricative consonant, heard in such words as vain, very vivid, roving, grave, etc. It is made by raising the jaw and placing the top front teeth on the lower lip and sending out the breath through the small aperture so formed. As the breath is sent into the mouth, a slight guttural action takes place before its emission into the fricative action for the production of the consonant. The contact of the teeth and the lip is relinquished by dropping the jaw which allows the free flow of the breath for the moulding of vowels. (V is allied to F as both are formed with the same articulatory action.)

W — The letter W is a peculiarity of the English language being, as it is, pronounced in different ways. It can be classified as a semi-vowel, an unvoiced consonant or a partially voiced consonant. For instance, in words such as wake,

THE HUMAN VOICE AS A MUSICAL INSTRUMENT

weep, worthy, wonderful, etc. it is presented as a semi-vowel due to the fact that the vowel o͞o is momentarily audible in its production. The sound of W, when appearing in words such as those just mentioned, is made by opening the mouth, then raising the jaw, contracting the cheeks and protruding the lips into a fairly small circular aperture. On sending out the breath the initial sound heard is that of the vowel o͞o. This must be immediately followed by a rapid drop of the jaw and relaxation of the cheeks and lips to enable the breath to flow freely for the moulding of vowels in the word to be made.

W – When W is followed in the spelling of words by ho, such as in who, whole, etc. It is produced and sounded as the unvoiced aspirated consonant H which is merely the escape of air passing through the open oral cavity, and the words who, whole, etc, are pronounced as hoo, hole, etc. For details of its formation, please refer back to the consonant H.

W – At other times when the consonant W is followed by the consonant h, for example in words such as what, wheel, where, etc. It is pronounced with the aspirate h being heard momentarily before it is moved very rapidly into the W, ie, sounding approximately as hoo-wer. It should be stated that some speakers no longer use this sound, preferring to sound only the W. The choice is entirely personal and in both cases acceptable as standard pronunciation. The writer considers it preferable to use WH when singing, being of the opinion that wot, weel, wear, would sound somewhat lacking in refinement. On the other hand, to over-emphasise the H would result in annoying affectation.

W – When occuring in words where it is followed by the consonant r, such as wraith, wreck, write, etc, it is not heard, merely the r is used, ie, ray-th, reck, rite.

W – In some cases where W occurs in the middle or endings of words it is unvoiced, for instance in jaw, sew, rowing, blowing, etc. On other occasions it modifies the preceeding vowel, as in new, how, jaw, ie, e-oo, ah-oo, or, etc. Care must be taken to ensure that it is not heard in such words.

X – This consonant is heard in different ways of pronunciation. In the middle and endings of words such as maximum, toxic, tax, lax, etc, it is heard as KS. In this instance it is formed by the combination of the implosive or stop consonant K, linked with the fricative consonant S as heard in such a word as wrecks. As the beginning of words such as xerox, xylophone, xiphoid, etc, it is heard precisely as the partially voiced fricative consonant Z, made by the tongue being placed with its front portion firmly pressed against the alveolar ridge. The breath issues through the narrow aperture thus formed with a buzzing sound in words such as zoom, zenith, zinc, etc.

DICTION

Y — Y is sometimes heard as a semi-vowel, at others as a short monophthong or in certain instances hardly discernible at all.

1) In such words as yet, yolk, yacht, youth, etc, it is termed a semi-vowel due to the fact that the vowel ē is heard momentarily in their commencement, which is produced in exactly the same manner as in a word like evil. The middle part of the tongue is arched so that it makes contact with the inside edges of the top teeth, with breath flowing freely through the somewhat narrow space in the oral cavity. The contact of the tongue with the teeth must be rapidly released for the onset of the vowel to be formed for the word to be made.

2) Where Y occurs in the middle of words such as crypt, mystic, nymph, etc, it is heard as the short monophthong vowel i̞ as in the word bit. For details of its formation please look under the vowel i̞, as in the word bit.

3) In the endings of words like lovely, jolly, etc, it is made almost indiscernible.

Z — Partially voiced lingua-palatal fricative consonant formed by placing the tip of the tongue behind the lower teeth, with the blade of the tongue behind slightly raised towards the alveolar ridge. The breath issues through the narrow aperture thus made in a buzzing sound heard in such words as zoom, zenith, zinc, etc. When occuring in the middle of words like razor, razzle, etc, it more resembles the sibilant sound of s, and similarly in the endings of words, for instance, in raze, maize when used in normal speech. (Z and S are allied consonants, both being formed with the same articulatory organs.)

PART 2

OBSERVATIONS ON THE TECHNIQUES OF SINGING

CHAPTER SEVEN

Phonation

This is the first aspect for consideration in the act of breathing – the onset of sound. It is essential that *musical* sound should always be the primary aim. Therefore the accuracy of the initial sound must always be foremost in our consideration; what follows is entirely dependent on its correct initiation.

In singing, the emission of sound is made possible by the breath impinging on the vocal folds, thus setting them in vibration. How this is done is of the utmost importance. The word ATTACK, often used to describe the onset of musical sound, is rather unfortunate as it tends to give the impression of some form of onslaught and force. It can be very misleading and dangerous. The act of phonation is far removed from any form of *attack* in that sense of the word.

The correct method to be used in commencing sound is by the use of what is termed THE STROKE OF THE GLOTTIS. As the term implies, it is the onset of sound made by the contact of the breath at the vocal folds, in a manner which will result in evenly balanced vibrations at all times in the varying levels of pitch and dynamic scope.

The stroke of the glottis is made possible by the ability of the ear to realise, first, the pitch of the initial note to be produced. This will enable, in a purely sensory manner (mental awareness), the necessary preparation of the vocal folds, accuracy of registration and use of the correct resonators. This is the mental state of preparation for phonation.

At the same time, the necessary action of the breathing muscles of inhalation must be realised to secure the correct air pressure and to ensure that its support is accurate for the action which is to follow.

At this stage compression will have been accomplished. This will bring about the state of readiness on the part of the breathing functions to commence phonation. MIND and BODY are now in synchronization and should work simultaneously.

The breath, which is now in a state of readiness, is *released* under the necessary suppressive control with the accurate momentum for the required pitch. It impinges on to the vocal folds in a gliding manner, so setting them in vibration, and sound emerges in a controlled tonal quality. It must be stressed that any attempt to control the breath by constriction at the chink of the glottis will result in disaster. The breath must flow freely except when *momentarily* partially or wholly impeded in the enunciation of words.

Here is a suggestion for practise to bring about the correct stroke of the glottis. Having made the mental and physical preparations, using the aspirated consonant h, make a very gentle onset of breath to the vocal folds, through the mouth and throat which are shaped for the formation of the vowel ah. Obviously no vocal sound will be heard as the air is escaping at the chink of the glottis, and therefore no vibrations are set up.

Now, WILLING the vocal folds to come into a state of proximity (analogy: as one *wills* the index finger and thumb to make the action of picking up a small object), produce the word WHO. The commencement of the vibrations of the folds will be clearly felt when the vowel o͞o is produced. Practise on *all* vowels in this manner.

Gradually shorten the duration of the h until no escape of air is audible, so starting the sound on the vowels immediately. The aim is to enable the onset of sound on words such as under, over, after, etc, with no kick of air at the glottis, but to start the vibrations of the vocal folds in a gliding or stroking manner.

When one is singing words which begin with consonants, especially those which are voiced, of course the act of phonation is much more easily accomplished.

Another method can be to hum the sound of n or l, on a single note in the medium register of the voice, being certain to leave the throat quite relaxed, followed by vowels and making words such as noon, north, lark, limp, etc.

Then make short word-phrases, singing them on the single note at first, and then making various small patterns of moving notes, for instances in a manner such as this:

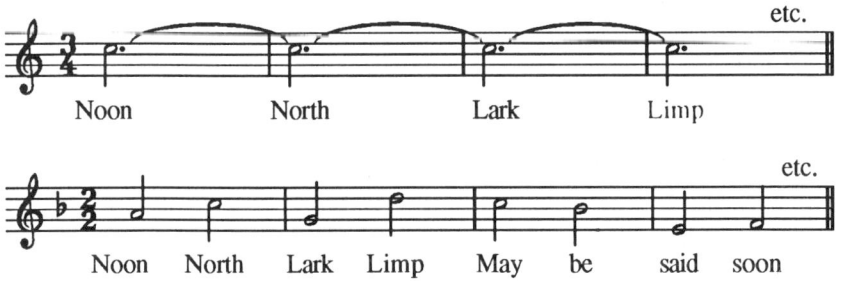

Great care must be taken in words beginning with sounds, such as go, king, carve. These can easily cause an attack at the glottis — termed a glottal attack.

The practise of vowel glides can also be used to good advantage. Take a deep breath and start singing a voiced consonant, for instance L, producing ah after it, then glide through a series of vowels, linking them all together. For example, something like this:

The correct act of phonation, that of the STROKE OF THE GLOTTIS, has been discussed. We must now become aware of some of the possible difficulties encountered in this aspect of voice production, the onset of vocal sound.

There can be no doubt that one of the most serious problems, and one which can cause great damage to the vocal folds, is that made by the use of the SHOCK OF THE GLOTTIS, sometimes termed GLOTTAL ATTACK. In this form of phonation the breath is sent with great force to the chink of the glottis, having a similar effect on the vocal folds, as occasioned by a cough or grunt.

There are various reasons for failure to ensure correct phonation in this instance. 1) There has been a lack of the necessary mental preparation, which should be made via the ear perceiving the required pitch and the correct placement of the note to be phonated. This preparation must be made to ensure that the vocal folds are accurately formed and conditioned to react in the proper manner as the breath impinges on them. 2) Not enough consideration has been given regarding correct registration and use of the complementary resonators before commencing phonation. 3) The inhalation of breath has possibly been made under too much force and in consequence brought about more compression than can be properly controlled by the breathing muscles, ie, intercostals, diaphragm and abdominal muscles. 4) Because of 3) above, the act of suppression has not been possible in the exhalation of the breath, so that it has been allowed to rush out with no accurate degree of restraint.

The result is that as the breath is expelled it makes a strenous onslaught on contacting the vocal folds, forcing them wide apart. As this forced action takes place there is a subconscious attempt on the part of the folds to regain some degree of proximity. On the recoil action, the inner edges of the vocal folds actually come into contact, striking one against the other.

Added to this, there is another attempt to obtain control by the contraction of the muscles at the chink of the glottis and in the larynx, pharynx and neck. Under these constricted conditions there can be little hope of the necessary control to enable proper phonation.

Eventually, if this 'attack' action continues, the texture of the vocal folds will become damaged by rough usage, and it will be necessary to take steps to hopefully restore them to a healthy condition, in which they can carry out their function in the correct manner. (For reference, see STROKE OF THE GLOTTIS)

The first sign of difficulties caused by glottal attack is the inability to glide into phonation, and it is found that the only possible way to commence phonation is to preceed the action with a glottal stop (as felt in articulating a word with a guttural consonant, ie, g or k). This forced contact at the chink of the glottis is so very often heard (and *felt* by the singer) in attempting a rising interval to the high register of the voice or commencing a phrase on that position in the compass. An unfortunate hoarse kind of 'crack' preceeds the onset of the tone which is very ugly to the ear and felt to be very distressing by the singer.

In remedial action, the first stage must be a good period of rest for the voice. The singer must accept the fact that the vocal folds have become very poor in their general condition owing to rough usage. They must therefore be allowed to have a chance to return to a normal and healthy condition by nature, just as a sore place or cut will heal if allowed to do so.

During this period of rest, which should be about three to four

PHONATION

weeks, all use of the voice should be minimal, even in speaking. When being used it should always be in a very gentle manner, and no singing should be undertaken.

When the vocal folds have been rested, some very gentle exercising may be attempted at the discretion of one's professor and, certainly, under his direction and advice, which is essential during this period of hopeful remedy.

All singers are inclined to HUM sounds, sometimes tunes. This is an excellent way in which to start to *feel* the return of the voice. Just hum n or m on an easy pitch and then, *very gently*, glide into a vowel, ensuring that no glottal stop is experienced. Then later, following the same example, undertake a small group of notes, say the first five notes of a major scale, ascending and descending, again in the easiest part of the voice. At first all practise should be done in the medium register of the voice. Gently moving passages such as those below may also be undertaken.

First, using mezzo forte sing each note on a vowel preceeded by a voiced consonant: lah, lah, lah ... etc. Then, grouping two or four notes together, use the voiced consonant only on the first note of each group. Something such as this, for example:

Lar - - - - - d   Lar - - - - - - - - - -d

Do not yet attempt exercises which *commence* on the higher notes in the voice; make a small pattern rising to the higher notes such as this:

Lah lah lah lah   lah lah   lah lah lah lah   lah

As is seen, the first three notes (a) leading to (b) should be sung in the high register of the voice so that there is no likelihood of the forcing of registers. (For reference, see BLENDING OF REGISTERS)

All notes should be sung at first with a voiced consonant preceeding the vowel, then on an open vowel starting with a voiced consonant used only on the first note.

Words may now be added to the pattern, such as these, for instance:

Simple songs which do not make any emotional or dramatic demands on the voice may now be introduced into practice. The compass must be very reasonable, the tessitura lying mostly in the medium register. There must be no sudden leaps in intervals, such as octaves and so on. The tempi also should be moderate.

Very gradually, as progress of recovery is made, there should be the attempt to return to normal working standard, but only when the new correct method of phonation is found to have been secured.

If, however, little or no improvement is experienced by taking these normal remedial steps, the possibility of trouble being caused by the formation of nodules on the vocal folds must be considered. These are minute corn-like proturberances which, if they do form, prevent the precise and accurate action of approximation. They are brought about by the ill use of the voice. If nodules are suspected, and especially if the trouble increases, the advice of a laryngologist should be sought immediately.

CHAPTER EIGHT

Breath control and legato singing

As it has been stated, it must be considered that breath control, in its many aspects, is a main function in singing. Nothing can be achieved without the motive power of the instrument. Only when the breath is under perfect control can there be any likelihood of a successful outcome from voice training.

This control lies in one direction: the mental and physical concentration in practising for development, and the dedication with which it is approached. One must THINK what one is endeavouring to achieve to ensure that the BRAIN is giving out the right messages to bring about the necessary PHYSICAL functions that must be produced. The MIND and BODY must always work in complete co-ordination.

The following suggestions for practice are designed to help students towards a sound understanding of the actions of the diaphragm and intercostal muscles in respiration, and to experience those actions. They can also further the sensations of compression and suppression.

Also it is essential to realise the importance of controlling the breath movement when changing registers. In moving from a lower to a higher register a corresponding increase of breath pressure must be made. In the reverse movement, from a higher to a lower register, the breath pressure must be correspondingly lessened. These changes in breath pressure are accomplished by the tensing and relaxation of muscles employed in breathing.

Suggestion in practice of this control in respiration:
1. Place one hand on the side of the rib cage at its base. Place the fingers of the other hand at the spot immediately under the base of the breast bone. In a panting fashion, inhale four short breaths through the open mouth and throat, the cavities of which are shaped as though to produce the vowel sound of ah. *Momentarily* hold the breath and then, in the same panting fashion, exhale the breath.

(An analogy: this will cause an action of the air similar to that produced when using fire bellows in four short detached movements.)

2. Repeat the intake of the breath as above. Now, without momentarily holding back the breath, immediately sing and sustain on an easy note the vowel o͞o or, if preferred, the word, moon. Continue to sing for as long as it is possible without causing any feeling of strain on the breathing muscles. There should be a good sense of rhythm by counting either three or four beats to the bar. The aim of practice in this manner is to increase gradually the sustaining ability of the breath. So, a few more bars may be added as progress is made. Also the tempo, which should be fairly *andante* at first, can be slowed down to encourage the controlling ability in *sostenuto* singing. Repeat as above using all vowel sounds in practice, and form and sing words using the various consonants. Add *crescendi* and *diminuendi* to increase dynamic scope. Small moving patterns can also be used either on an open vowel sound or in words.

3. Without inhaling by the panting method, take in a deep breath and, singing, sustain a word. Use all kinds of consonants and vowels to produce a variety of words. Also the words can be linked together to form a phrase. Gradually increase the sustaining ability by adding more bars, words, and phrases.

Be sure that all control of breath is made by the respiratory and supporting muscles. There must never be the slightest feeling of control by the constriction of the muscles of the neck, throat, mouth, tongue and jaw.

Legato singing

The aim of all musicians must be to establish a firm LEGATO line. It is from this ability that all good musical performances stem. In singing, such an ability is made possible by the accurate and controlled action of the breathing apparatus to ensure the balance of compression and suppression of the breath in its emission as it impinges on the vocal folds, thus setting them in vibration. In addition to developing breath control in the above suggested manner, practice for legato singing must also be undertaken by using slow scales, arpeggi, intervals, etc, and, of course, later by very sustained pieces.

Movements such as this, for example, should be found very beneficial:

BREATH CONTROL AND LEGATO SINGING

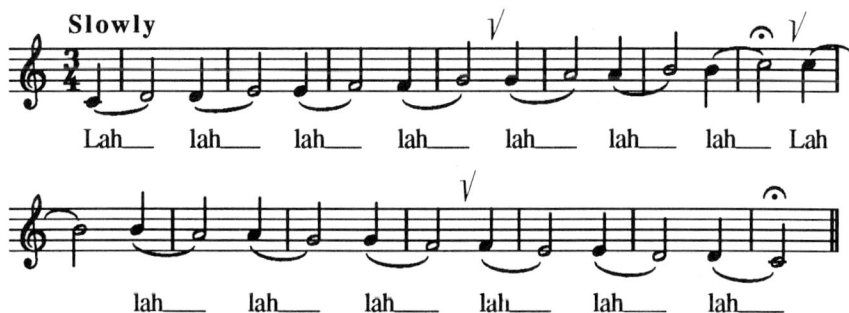

Practice fairly slowly at first, taking breaths as indicated; then later, as control is developed, dispense with the breaths other than the one at the top of the scale before descending. The same tone levels, ie, from 'p' to 'f', should be maintained in practising. As the ability to sustain a legato line is developed, the speed may be made slower and slower, so calling for more and more breath control.

Some useful songs for practise in legato singing are:

Fairly easy: *Caro mio ben* (Giordani)
Moderately difficult: *O del mio dolce ardor* (Gluck)
Difficult: *Care selve* (Handel)

CHAPTER NINE

Phrasing

A wise motorist before setting out on a journey, whether it be a short or a long one, will have become familiar with the route to be taken. Consideration will have been given to places en route where fuel can be obtained.

The wise singer will, in studying the musical journey, give priority to where, in the phrasing, breath may be replenished according to the sense and punctuation of the music and the words.

The petrol tank can, as required, be completely refilled or just topped up; breath can be replenished by full breaths, or short ones, which we will call 'snatched' breaths.

In most cases, and wherever possible, full breaths in replenishment must be taken. The inhalation of these are, as we already know, brought about by the combined action of diaphragmatic and intercostal breathing. At times when big, sustained phrases are encountered in music of a florid style, it may be found necessary to take breaths although no break in the continuity of the musical movement is indicated. In such phrases there is usually plenty of time to take in full breaths at some point or another without interrupting the word-sense or punctuation. But great attention must be paid to this aspect. Here is an excerpt from *With Verdure Clad* from Haydn's *Creation*, with suggested phrasing:

PHRASING

However, at times, where the movement of the music calls for fast tempi and where long, quick passages occur, there may not be enough time to take in full breaths, and one has to snatch a top-up breath very quickly.

Development of the ability to take snatched breaths will be aided by practising as follows. Sing a series of short repeated notes, comfortably pitched to suit the voice, using a vowel preceeded by a voiced consonant on *each* note; for instance, lah or law. Do not breathe until the sustained notes are reached, and then snatch in a breath very quickly:

Gradually increase the number of repeated notes to encourage sustained and controlled breathing.

Next, sing a sustained note, mentally counting the bars, say four to start with. This time only use a voiced consonant on the very first note, continuing on only the vowel throughout. Again snatch a breath as indicated and lengthen the duration of the sustained note. Gradually increase the number of bars on which the note is sustained to encourage breath control.

It must be the ultimate aim of all singers to maintain breath throughout long phrases and in agile movements in which lengthy runs occur. However, sometimes this may not be possible in the early stages of singing. For instance, it might be very difficult for a young singer to accomplish all the runs in *Every Valley*, from *Messiah*. Here, and in many other instances, it is most likely that snatched breaths will have to be employed if the movement is to be kept up to the correct tempo.

There are also instances in many songs where snatched breaths need to be used. For instance, in *Five Eyes* (Armstrong Gibbs) and *Mother Carey* (Frederic Keel) there are continuous words in the lyrics with no apparent space for the taking of breaths, and one has to snatch in a breath wherever possible. Needless to add, it must be done in a manner where neither word punctuation nor musical phrasing are adversely affected. It must also be remembered that snatched breaths must be accomplished in a quick but gentle manner, avoiding any fierce inhalation.

CHAPTER TEN

Agility

A most important requirement of any singer is the ability to control the many demands encountered in music which call for agility. By agility the writer means the ability to move the voice quickly and evenly in fast-moving runs or quick passages, ornamentations, cadenzas, etc, which appear so frequently in operas and oratorios, and, of course in many songs. For instance, one can find such examples in *The Creation* (Haydn), *Messiah* (Handel), *Exultate Jubilate* (Mozart), *Il Barbiere di Siviglia* (Rossini), *Die Zauberflöte* (Mozart), and so on.

At times the term 'florid' is used in describing agility and seems to cause some confusion. For the bass voice, the writer suggests a piece such as *The Trumpet shall sound* (especially the second section) in *Messiah* (Handel), the soprano solo *With Verdure Clad* from *The Creation* (Haydn) and the song by Mozart, *Ridente la Calma*, as being florid – certainly not agile – but demanding great *flexibility* in movement.

In the early stages of training, the development of control in agility may be found to present some difficulties. As the term implies, it is the controlled execution of music containing fast runs, arpeggi, cadenzas, and so on.

It is also necessary to be able to maintain the indicated tempi in the movements. This very often presents much difficulty in the early stages. Many times a young singer has been heard to say 'I'll practise the runs slowly to begin with and then later, speed up to the correct tempo.' Yes, slowly at first, for one reason only: to ensure that the notation is accurate.

There are various ways in which by practise, patience and perseverance, controlled agility can be accomplished. Here is an example: take a passage from the aria *Rejoice greatly*, for the soprano voice, in Handel's *Messiah*, and approach it as follows:

First take the 'skeleton', or main notes, on which the passage is written. It will be seen that they are as follows:

Now dissect the group of notes into small sections, and sing *every* note on a vowel preceeded by a voiced consonant (lah, lah, lah, for instance). Use whichever consonant and vowel preferred. Remember that the correct tempo must be maintained in each group. The groups are indicated thus ⌐─∨─∨─┐ etc. Make a slight break at the end of each group and then commence the next group:

Now link two groups together; repeat as above but use only one consonant at each commencing point, using a slight emphasis there, after the breaks. Now link all the groups together, using only the word 'rejoice' as printed, so making the whole passage complete.

Such a method can be applied in all similar instances. Eventually, it will give the young singer *something* concrete on which to build individual security, and a technique which will bring about a satisfactory result. It is very doubtful that the 'sing it slowly' approach will have the same effect. In the above mentioned example, providing the run is performed at the correct speed, there will be no need for a breath to be taken; it can easily be sung in one phrase.

Take another example. A pattern such as this one taken from *Every Valley* (*Messiah*):

AGILITY

In this particular instance, and all others where the pattern of the run includes tied notes, there should be no difficulty in the intake of breath. One just shortens, very slightly of course, the note on which the tie ends and snatches in a breath. It is for the singer to choose at what point the breath is taken, but it should be at points equally spaced in the overall number of bars taken up by the run.

However, in some cases where there is no such ready-made point at which to take in breath, for instance in such examples as follows (Mozart's *Exultate Jubilate*), it may then become necessary to contrive a place where *momentarily* there may be a very slight break to snatch a breath:

Another example (opposite) is from Bach's B minor Mass.

Remember in agile movements that whilst all the notes must be clearly articulated, they must be smooth and lightweight. The tone must be buoyant and poised. Any attempt to give too much weight in tone will result in very laboured and ponderous singing, and make speed and agility very difficult or even impossible. Unless there is call for some dramatic emphasis, the use of very strong accentuation in runs is not acceptable, neither is the employment of the 'intrusive H', which is an easy way out, but not good technique.

AGILITY

CHAPTER ELEVEN

Blending of the registers

An essential aspect of voice production which must be fully understood is that of the blending of the registers. In the development of the necessary technique in this respect, the use of VOWEL GLIDES (a technique which is also used in other aspects of singing, that of legato singing and achieving clarity in words) will be found to be of great assistance.

By their employment in practise, the sensations of the smooth movements necessary between registers should be experienced, as will be seen later. But first, a very simple example:

Gently sustaining a single note at a comfortable pitch in the medium register of the voice, sing a vowel – for instance aw, preceeded by the voiced consonant, say l, to enunciate the word 'law'. Keeping a firm rhythm, gently *glide* into the vowel ē, again preceeding it with the consonant l, so as to enunciate the word 'lean'. Now return to the word 'law'. Make no break between them, use the sung consonant l to link them together. This action is termed a vowel glide. All combinations of vowels may be used in practise, increasing the number of bars as necessary:

In this manner of practice, the sensations of a slight change in the area of resonance will be experienced in the gradual, gliding change from the vowel or/aw (which may be felt to be emanating with mostly phraynx and mouth resonance) to the vowel ē, there will be felt and heard a slightly more 'frontal' or 'forward' positioning of the tone in the area of the nasopharynx. Also there will possibly be noticed a slight alteration in the timbre of the voice. Both are correct and to be welcomed.

BLENDING OF THE REGISTERS

Now, carrying out the same rhythmic movement, the number of bars may be increased in the exercise and the vowels may be varied, for instance:

At first make use of a voiced consonant, eg, l, m, n, ng, etc, before the various vowels to assist a smooth movement from one to another. Later, endeavour must be made to dispense with this aid and still maintain the same vocal flow in singing words which do not all commence with voiced consonants, thus:

This form of practice may now be used again, this time singing the notes at different pitches.

In the early stages of the development in the technique necessary for correct blending of the registers, especially in the female voices, it is wise to commence practising on small passages which move *down*. This will assist in ensuring that no forcing of the registers will be made, which can happen if in practice passages always ascend, thereby bringing about the possibility of, for instance, carrying the medium register too high. Practice such as follows may be undertaken to advantage. Use keys suitable for individual voice categories. Maintain the sensation of the high register for the first phrase, then the medium register for the second phrase. Repeat without taking a breath and blend the high and medium registers together, gliding from one to the other, ensuring there is no gap between them. Practise on all vowels.

OBSERVATIONS ON THE TECHNIQUES OF SINGING

Some further suggestions may now be undertaken which will also aid achievement in the blending of the registers:

1. Ascend and descend on the first five notes of a major scale, covering a point necessitating a change of register. Start the scale *mezzo forte*, and *diminuendo* on the ascent to the fifth note. Make a short pause there, and then descend to the starting point, making a slight *crescendo* to *mezzoforte* towards the end of the scale. Sing the scale on a vowel preceeded by the consonant t on *each* note. It is suggested that the vowel o͞o, as in the word 'noon', should be used: too, too, too, too, too, etc. This seems to be most suitable for the purpose in the beginning, which is to *sense* the movement of tone into a more 'forward' position in the area of the nasopharynx resonation in the ascending scale, and to return to the lower resonance of the descending notes. Practice later in the various register-positions suitable to the voice categories but do not attempt any extremes as yet.

For instance, the soprano voice can be practised around an area in the compass such as follows:

and similar positions can be applied in the compasses of the various voice categories.

As the point of such practice is realised (which is to bring about a smooth transition from one tessitura to another) and progress is made in experiencing the sensations of controlling the movements, practice should be undertaken as follows:

2. Using the same five-note scale system, sing up *slowly* on sustained notes, using a long vowel such as aw, as in the word 'more', and gradually blend it into the vowel oo as in the word 'moon' as the higher notes are reached. On the descent, continuing on the oo sound, gradually blend back to the aw sound to finish the scale:

BLENDING OF THE REGISTERS

Other groupings of notes, used in the same manner, may be introduced, for instance:

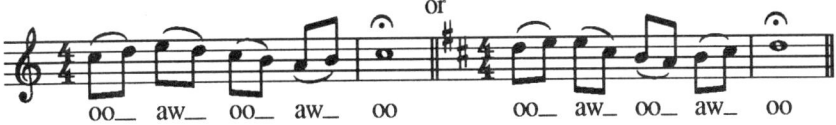

In fact, any small movement weaving around the changing areas of registration which will encourage the sensations of blending the registers, together with the blending of the areas of resonation, which must also be fully realised, will prove very advantageous. Such practising as in the foregoing should enable the singer to experience the sensations of registration quite clearly.

3. Practise combining scales and arpeggi movements should now be undertaken. Using the same method of starting with a voiced consonant on the first note, as suggested previously (later it will be necessary to commence the exercises without this aid), blending vowels such as aw to ōo, ah to ē, etc, sing an ascending major scale of one octave. Start the scale on a broad sound such as aw, ah, and gradually blend into ōo, ē, on the way up. Make a *slight* pause on the top note of the scale, and then descend on the arpeggio, 5.3.1 of the scale, blending back into the broad sound on which the scale was started. This should be practiced slowly so that the sensations of the blending of the registers and vowel-shaping can be more easily experienced:

4. Ascending and descending scales, major and both forms of minor, melodic and harmonic. It is suggested that at first major scales of nine notes should be used. Later the scales may be extended, step by step, until they cover, say, an octave and five notes, using the method of placing a voiced consonant before the vowel at the points of rhythmic emphasis. Practice should be done at all speeds. Arppegi in any form, using the above method of execution, should be undertaken. First a very simple one, such as a major chord arpeggi:

OBSERVATIONS ON THE TECHNIQUES OF SINGING

As progress is made, using the various blendings of the vowels, practice in the style that follows may be undertaken:

Later such practising should be sung on *one* vowel sound without the aid of voiced consonants in starting them.

5. It is essential that intervals can be accomplished in a secure technique, and practise must be undertaken to ensure the development of this ability. In the early stages, the practise of small simple intervals, such as major thirds, perfect fourths and fifths, will suffice. These should be practised in the medium part of the particular voice category. Later they should be undertaken in just the small area of the overall compass of the voice where the transition from one register to another is necessary. Eventually, bigger demands will have to be met where intervals of much greater pitches occurs, and which will have to be accomplished with technical security.

The following method of approach to the secure ability of interval singing, by the assurance that the sensation of the blending of the registers is experienced, is suggested:

Employing rising and falling intervals, use a broad vowel, such as ah, on the lower note and, moving on a slow *portamento di voce* (carried on the voice), glide into a more closed/forward vowel, such as o͞o, for the higher note, returning to ah to finish on the lower note.

Preceed each vowel with a voiced consonant, such as l, m, n, which will help to move without gaps or breaks occuring between the notes. For instance:

BLENDING OF THE REGISTERS

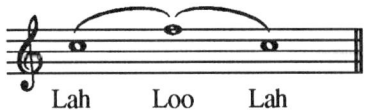

Lah   Loo   Lah

Make the movement as *legato* as possible and give a dynamic of 'mf' on the lower note, making a *diminuendo* to the higher one and returning to 'mf' to finish.

Eventually, of course, one must be able to accomplish intervals of every quality, and this without the aid of either the use of *portamento* or voiced consonant. This will necessitate the gradual *discontinuance* of such aids in practise, so that the biggest interval can be negotiated on an open vowel sound, or words when required, with complete control.

Here is a demonstration of the blending of registers suggested in an actual excerpt from *With Verdure Clad*, an aria for the soprano voice from *The Creation* by Haydn:

It will be seen that bars 1, 2 and 3 lie in the medium register. However, to ensure a controlled movement into the higher register in bars 4, 5, 6, 7 and the rise to the pause in bar 8, the singer must not use the medium register completely for those first three bars. These must be sensed as belonging to the top note of the medium register, ie, E flat.

Unless this is realised, ie, feeling always that one is moving towards the higher register and blending the medium register with it, there will be some difficulties encountered at bars 4 and 5, and especially bars 6 and 7, where the voice has to float to the pause in bar 8. If only the quality of the medium register is used in the first three bars in the areas of the B flats and Cs, there will most likely have to be a sudden register change at the F in bar 4. By the continued blending of the two registers, the three lines can always be poised and secure. Naturally the functions of the breathing muscles will have to be fully realised in the varying breath pressures, and the control of compression and suppression must be made to ensure the necessary support. The voice can of course come into the medium register to finish at bars 9, 10 and 11.

The following is an excerpts from the third of the *Vier Letzte Lieder* by Richard Strauss:

This is a very good illustration of the necessity of the blending of the registers. The singer here must maintain the tessitura of the high notes — those marked with asterisks — using the high register throughout the phrases until the last two notes. Should the voice be allowed to drop into a lower register at those points, most likely a 'change of gear' would result and a very marked difference in tonal quality would be heard.

Sometimes difficulties may be caused by sudden forced movement in intervals. If one is singing in the medium register of the voice and is called upon to move, by a big interval, into a higher register, a break in continuity can easily occur if the technique of the blending of registers is not secure. In such a passage as follows, the singer

BLENDING OF THE REGISTERS

must practise gradually preparing to make the required movement in registration at places marked a, b, c, d to avoid the sudden changes:

The first five notes should be gradually changing towards the higher tessitura of (a). Now, they must *remain* at this level until again, by feeling a slight lift in the tone, (b) has been reached. The next three notes must remain in the high tessitura until (c) is reached, and ditto, until arriving at (d). Very gently the last three notes are floated into the lower tessitura. This should ensure that there are no ups and downs in the single *notes*, but that one is thinking in 'planes' or 'levels' for the *groups* of notes. (Analogy: one can play groups of notes in the compass of an octave on the keyboard, sometimes more, without making a movement of the wrist. But if it is played with *one* finger, eight movements have to be made.)

One must, of course, ensure that correct resonation is employed in the various levels or planes (tessitura) which are called for.

The forcing of registers will cause serious damage to the voice. It usually occurs in rising intervals. It is especially encountered in young singers, who have perhaps undertaken a performance of works where emotional and dramatic contents in texts and music demand more than they are able to produce with control. But also the fault is sometimes heard in mature singers who have, through carelessness and lack of mental and vocal concentration, taken a chance and 'had a go' at those climaxes and high notes, with disastrous results!

It is brought about by the misguided and dangerous endeavour to produce more tone by pushing and straining the voice. The most usual defect is where the singer, in an attempt to add more weight and intensity to the tone, tries to do so by carrying the deeper quality of the medium register into the higher register with no thought to the necessity of BLENDING them from one to the other. This results from a lack of adjustments in the vocal folds and the absence of appreciation for the correct resonation. The outcome is a desperate, unhappy *shout*, in an attempt to reach a higher tessitura, and almost certainly, in the case of intervals necessitating changes from one register to another, a break in the voice. Due to this forcing and

OBSERVATIONS ON THE TECHNIQUES OF SINGING

overtaxing of the tone, the intonation will be insecure and result in flatness in pitch. Practise must be undertaken in the blending of registers.

Also one can overtax a voice and cause vocal collapse if one persistently sings music which lies in the wrong tessitura for the particular voice; for instance, where a lyric soprano endeavours to sing music which is written for the coloratura range, or a bass undertakes music which lies for a good deal of the time in the higher range of the voice.

Troubles can also arise by singers undertaking music which is not suitable for their particular vocal qualities and which makes tonal demands beyond reason.

CHAPTER TWELVE

Good tonal production

Good tonal production is dependent on many aspects of voice production. The following functions play a most important part: the control of breathing, the accuracy of the use of the registers of the voice, combined with the correct technique of resonation and the correct use of the speech organs employed in diction. Of especial importance in the development of accuracy is the moulding of the vowels. This has a tremendous bearing on the resultant colour and quality of the tone.

Added to these faculties is the great part played by the sensations which the singer experiences in using the voice: the ability to differentiate between what *feels* good or bad when producing the tone. In training, an inexplicable sense of right and wrong should develop as progress is made, and every encouragement should be given to this aspect in discussion between student and professor.

The act of phonation has already been discussed, when it was seen that the adjustments in the tensions and approximations of the vocal folds necessitate accuracy to ensure good onset of tone.

In tone which is termed 'breathy' the vocal folds are not properly prepared for phonation. The chink of the glottis is not formed accurately: the space between the vocal folds is too wide and their tensions in the various areas of registration are not being correctly adjusted. It will also be found that the middle notes of the voice (the medium register) are sometimes very weak. It is possible that the functions of the breathing muscles are not fully under control and the necessary support is not being given. The resulting tone will be very veiled and dull in quality and lack projection.

Practise to experience the correct approximations and tensions of the vocal folds must be undertaken.

For instance, sing a series of repeated staccato notes, very gently, on a vowel preceeded by the unvoiced consonant 'the hard C' on an easy pitch in the medium register of the voice. The vowel o͞o is suggested to start with, so producing the word 'coo'. All vowels should be practised eventually. Do not take in breaths between each staccato note: link them together, as it were, on a sustained breath line so that the 'clip' of the 'k' sound can be easily felt each time the word 'coo' is started. This will prove that the correct action of the vocal folds is taking place:

Coo, coo, coo, coo, coo, coo, coo, coo, coo, coo, coo, coo, coo, coo, coo, coo, coo.

Now sing in the same manner, repeated staccato notes in various pitches in the overall compass of the voice, but be reasonable and do not attempt extremes. When the actions of approximation and tension are clearly experienced, dispense with the hard C and practise the technique of the stroke of the glottis as discussed in the section on PHONATION. Practise should be undertaken to make it possible to commence words such as 'over', 'enter', 'on', 'after', etc, with a clean, crisp tone in the onset with no suggestion of a glottal shock.

If the passage of tone into the mouth is obstructed by the root of the tongue being pushed up by constricted muscular action, so coming into contact with the soft palate, the resulting tone will be colourless and nasal in quality. The tone is unable to flow out through the buccal cavity and can only emerge through the nasal passages. To eliminate this error of tone production, practise singing on a note on the consonant ng with an open mouth, gliding from it into open sounds such aw, ah, ā. As this transition is made it will produce the free flow of tone in the correct manner, with accurate resonance and quality, due to the fact that the main cavities of resonation – the pharynx, the mouth and the nasopharynx – are being fully employed in their accurate proportions. The use of the ng consonant is to ensure that the tone will have the necessary nasal *resonance* (not to be confused with *nasal tone*) in the combination of other resonating areas to give the projection of the tone.

Here is another simple manner in which it is possible to experience the feeling of freedom at the back of the mouth and to differentiate between nasal *tone* and the correct emission of tone which has nasal *resonance*:

GOOD TONAL PRODUCTION

With the mouth open and shaped to form the vowel ah, breathe in through the nose. It will be easily felt that the back part of the tongue and the soft palate come into contact with each other as this action is made, so making it impossible for breath to be drawn into the buccal cavity (it *can* be done but with the sound of a snore ensuing !!) Now send out the breath through the mouth, singing the word 'car'. A small click will be felt and heard between the soft palate and the root of the tongue because this action will cause them to part company. The tone will now be able to flow freely through the mouth.

Much faulty tone may be traced to the area of the root of the tongue and soft palate. If the root of the tongue is bunched up and the soft palate is pushed down it will affect the quality of the tone very badly – it will be very 'throaty' and sound forced. Great attention must be given in early training to ensure that the passage for the tone is always free except when, momentarily, it is impeded for the articulation of guttural consonants.

Poor tonal production may be brought about as a result of constriction of the muscles of the larynx, pharynx and areas of the nasopharynx. Such a constriction causes the narrowing of the aperture from the phraynx into the buccal cavity, thus preventing a free flow of air and the production of spacious tone. This is a common fault associated with trying to control the breath at the chink of the glottis, instead of correctly effecting breath control via compression and suppression, using only the muscles employed in breathing. Some different ways by which the above-mentioned constriction of muscles could arise and possible ways of remedying these faults are suggested.

In the production of good tonal quality the larynx should be positioned as it is in everyday ordinary normal breathing, and the pharynx will be spacious, as in the act of yawning. If, however, in the act of singing the larynx rises and the pharynx takes on the feeling of *stifling* a yawn, the resulting tone will be what is known as 'throaty' or 'guttural'. As the term suggests, this is a sound produced with gripped muscular constriction of the area of the soft palate and the back of the tongue, causing the opening into the buccal cavity to become very small and in a squeezed-up state. The sides of the tongue at its back part will be felt to be making contact with the inside edges of the back teeth. There will be little resonance, and what there may be will be mostly confined to the throat, being very ugly in quality.

OBSERVATIONS ON THE TECHNIQUES OF SINGING

If the muscles at the root of the tongue are constricted, the tongue will be into a humped-up position at the back of the mouth, almost coming into contact with the soft palate. This will lead to production of a so-called 'tight' or 'rigid' tone which will lack colour and quality.

To remedy the above faults, practice must be undertaken to bring about relaxation of the constricted muscles, namely those of the tongue itself, the muscles that enter the tongue from the various areas of the mouth, especially those connected with the tongue bone (HYOID BONE) and those of the neck. Attention must also be paid in ensuring that there is no stiffening of the jaw, which will also contribute to the troubles mentioned.

Suggested practice which should help is as follows: sing the word 'yarn', repeatedly on a monotone, allowing the tongue to lie flat in the base of the mouth and the jaw to drop loosely and naturally. By placing the fingers and the thumb around the thyroid cartilage (the Adam's Apple), one can tell if there are any tensions in this region of the throat by feeling whether the thyroid cartilage is rising up or not. In a tension-free throat, it should lie in the normal position it takes on when breathing quietly using mouth respiration.

Another aid that can also be used to advantage is the act of yawning. This is an excellent means whereby to experience the space and relaxation that is possible in that area of the vocal instrument. All singers should indulge in this exercise by either simulating a yawn or, better still, by *actually* yawning. With the mouth and throat formed in the position of an onset of a yawn, sound the nasal consonant ng, ensuring that the thyroid cartilage does not rise up, and then move into the vowel ah. It is possible that, by practise, this exercise can be done with no tension in the muscles already mentioned above, so that one can actually sing the word 'yarn' with complete freedom from the above faults. It is of course necessary to practise on all the vowels, so that they can all be produced with the same ease and relaxation.

If one wishes to see the actual physical action of the root of the tongue and the soft palate, take a mirror, stand in good light so that a view into the back of an open mouth is made possible. The above actions can now be visually observed.

A number of causes contribute to the serious fault of unsteady tone, a TREMOLO, the dreaded 'wobble'. This is a wavering tone, causing the effect of a fluctuating pitch.

GOOD TONAL PRODUCTION

Amongst the causes of the unsteadiness in the emission of vocal tone, and one most likely to be found, is that of some defect in breath control, ie, the accurate balance of compression and suppression which ensures a controlled inhalation and exhalation of breath. However, it must be appreciated that slight adjustments of the balance are necessitated in alterations of tessitura.

There may be too much breath pressure in the singing or, on the other hand, a lack in the support sufficient to ensure steady flow of tone in the singing.

Other reasons for the wobble can be the misuse of the registers. Forcing them will, as it has been seen, bring about serious trouble. The use of excessive volume, trying to sing too loudly, too much emphasis in phonation, bringing about 'glottal attack' – these are some of the factors that play a part in unsteady tone. Pitch will also suffer, possibly resulting in flat singing.

Also, the performing of works which are not really suitable for the particular vocal qualities of the individual voice will present trouble in control. Much attention should be paid in this direction to ensure that the tessitura of the music does not bring about any strain on the voice.

In any endeavour to rectify *tremolo*, the correct use in the techniques of phonation, registration and volume control should be continually observed in practice.

The practice of MESSA DI VOCE should prove helpful:

First, singing quite softly, sustain a single note in an easy part of the medium register, at a dynamic level in which no unsteadiness occurs. Then very gradually practice to increase the amount of volume, but only to the degree which still ensures steadiness. With practise it should be possible to add more and more volume until reasonable contrasts in the dynamic levels are possible. It must be understood that the exercise 'Messa di voce' is a gradual crescendo ⊂ and diminuendo ⊃ so one must not stay at the peak of the crescendo in practise, but must finish the exercise by returning to the soft dynamic level on which the exercise was commenced.

Later the practice may be done at varying pitches in the overall compass of the voice and also using scale passages and arpeggi. In using messa di voce, ensure that no constriction is being put on the muscles of the larynx, pharynx and neck, causing strain at the chink of the glottis.

OBSERVATIONS ON THE TECHNIQUES OF SINGING

Tremolo should not be confused with VIBRATO, which is an asset, apparent in all good voices. It is a gentle quiver or regular oscillation of the tone which yet, fundamentally, remains quite steady. It is a natural attribute to the tone and has no adverse effect on pitch. It is more clearly audible in the higher reaches of the voice and in higher levels of dynamics. No attempt should be made to 'cultivate' it; it will most likely end in a wobble if one does so. It should appear quite naturally, with general development, in potentially promising voices.

Placing or placement of tone is a term used in connection with voice production to illustrate to students that, by sensation, tone can be produced with the right qualities of resonance.

It does no harm, as has been stated previously, to allow them to *imagine* tone being produced in various areas of the vocal instrument, ie, chest, mouth, head, etc, but it must be emphasised that it should always be born in mind that sound is produced by the breath vibrating the vocal folds, which is only possible at their situation in the instrument of the voice, ie, at the chink of the glottis and *not* in the chest, *not* in the head, etc.

The tone should always emerge from that area just behind the front top teeth. This will ensure that all the main cavities of resonation, ie, pharynx, nasopharynx and mouth, and in the lower pitches, the chest, are being used in combination, to the various degrees required for any given pitch. This will ensure good projection of the tone.

For instance, if the tone were to emerge with only mouth resonation, the tone would be very veiled and dull. On the other hand, if by allowing the soft palate and tongue to meet, nasal tone will result as it could only emerge through the nose.

Unless the various areas of resonation are combined in their right proportions, the resulting tone will not be accurate. If the tone lacks the resonation which is produced by the employment of the nasopharynx, there is little possibility of its having projection of the right intensity. It will not reach further than the first few rows of seats in the auditorium.

Tone which has well projected quality is sometimes termed 'frontal' tone. This is because the sensations of the correct use of the resonating cavities in the area of the nasopharynx are experienced by the singer. However, great care must be taken to ensure that *nasal tone* does not result by any misunderstanding of the difference between this and nasal resonance, which is essential.

GOOD TONAL PRODUCTION

The cause of tone which lacks projection is that it is emerging with too much emphasis from the cavities of the pharynx and mouth, and quite 'missing' the route via the area of the nasopharynx which is necessary to complete the combination of the three resonators, pharynx, mouth and nasopharynx.

Practice should be undertaken to ensure good tonal projection. For instance, sing a small series of staccato notes using short vowels on words such as 'song', 'sing', 'sang' in the following fashion: sing each note staccato and then sustain the ng on the last note. This will encourage the sensation of resonance in the area of the naso-pharynx:

Now sing an ascending major scale of an octave in the same manner, make a small pause on the top note, during which the ng is turned into a vowel, ie, ah, ē, aw, etc, and descend the scale singing on the vowel. Glide from the ng into the vowel, do not make a sudden change, so causing a glottal stop:

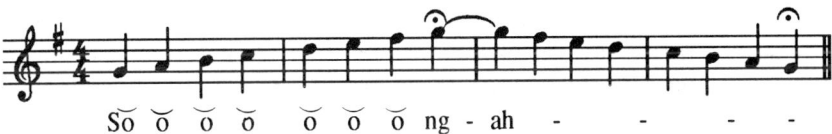

Practice singing gentle staccato notes – a series on one note will do – in various positions of pitch on the more forward vowels, ie, ē, ĕ, ĭ, etc. Pinch the nostrils while doing this exercise to ensure that *nasal tone* is not being produced.

Sing reasonable intervals (say fourths, fifths, sixths) first in one register – the medium one is best for a start – and then some which necessitate the change from one register to another. Commence on the lower note with a long vowel and glide into a short one on the higher note, ie, ah to ē, returning to ah on descending the scale. Words can be introduced into practice using the same method, for instance, 'Lords of Lords', etc. Bigger intervals can now be undertaken, some which move between the medium and higher register.

OBSERVATIONS ON THE TECHNIQUES OF SINGING

In all cases, ensure that the tone retains the senation of nasopharynx resonance and does not slip away from it at any time:

If the speech organs of articulation are not correctly used or the formation of the resonating cavities are not accurately moulded for the production of vowels, the singer's diction and also the tone will certainly not be good.

On occasion it has been stated in connection with voice production that 'at all times when singing the tongue must lie flat on the floor of the mouth'. Certainly the root of the tongue must not be allowed to rise and stiffen and become bunched up at the back of the mouth, so preventing the freedom of the flow of tone into the buccal cavity. However, it must be able to move quite freely in the mouth and certainly to alter in shape and position. Without this freedom, good diction will be impossible and also the quality of tone would suffer in consequence.

If one sings the vowel ah, then the tongue should lie flat and will do so, as one would suppose, quite naturally. Now, leaving the tongue in that position, attempt a word with the vowel ā as in the word 'pay' or the word 'weep', and immediately the tone is very distorted. And so it is obvious that the tongue must be used in many shapes and positions when singing, not only for the means of good diction but also to enable good tonal qualities. In the case of lip formations, necessary in words such as, for instance, dawn, pull, too, as well as the different shapes at the lips, the tongue will again have to alter in position and shape. As far as consonants are concerned, the tongue must be formed into many shapes if the words are to be articulated correctly. The *tip* of the tongue is used extensively, for instance, in words such as look, too, the rolled r as in roar and round, etc. In words where guttural consonants are used, such as good, crow, etc, it can easily be felt that the *root* of the tongue rises towards the soft palate, which descends to start the word.

At this point, attention is drawn to the correct combined uses of the tongue, lips and all the other organs of speech which have been

GOOD TONAL PRODUCTION

described in detail in the alphabet chart contained in Chapter 6. The problem of bad vocal tone caused by incorrect use of the speech organs can be tackled by studying the instructions contained in the above-mentioned chart given for the proper and accurate moulding of vowels and the clear articulation of consonants. The accomplishment of the latter will not only enable good enunciation of words but will also enhance the production of good tone. Diction (the making and enunciation of words) and good tonal production are inextricably linked and it is essential that this relationship is not overlooked when attempting to deal with problems concerning a singer's tonal qualities.

PART 3

GENERAL ADVICE

CHAPTER THIRTEEN

'What type of voice do I have?'
Classification of voices and natural range

All voices start to show their natural quality early in training, and it is from this natural sound that they can eventually be classified. However, this takes time, due to the fact that in training some changes *may* occur in physical development. An open mind in making any final decision must therefore be kept until such time as definite trends in quality are shown. Nowadays, due to the laryngoscope, a laryngologist may possibly be able to give an opinion as to a classification if desired to do so. Some vocal folds show tendency towards a particular type of voice, due to their being either thin, short, thick, long, etc, in comparison to others. For instance, a high lyric soprano quality would probably be produced by a woman with fairly thin folds. On the other hand, the folds as a *real* contralto would possibly be rather thicker. But, eventually, the voice itself will find its true classification, by showing its true tonal quality and overall range as development is continued.

A word here on the mezzo voice. Many times it has been heard said by very young female singers 'I am a contralto.' In many cases, this may be accounted for by the fact that *some* of the girls in school choirs *have* to undertake the lower parts in the score (mostly the ones with good enough ears and musicianship to maintain the parts that are not the 'tune'!), and therefore imagine that, having used only the lower part of the voice in early life, there is nothing higher up to be developed.

In the long experience of the writer, most of the young 'contraltos'

GENERAL ADVICE

develop into mezzos and, in quite a lot of cases, dramatic sopranos. The numbers of those who prove to have time contralto voices are very small. However, it must be remembered that there *are* roles in oratorio and opera that are given the designation 'contralto', and so our mezzos must take on that title as required.

All voices have a natural range, at first sometimes very limited – perhaps just over one octave. There can be an idea that by 'pushing the breath harder it will push the voice higher' (rather like pushing a sweep's brush up the chimney!). This is, of course, a very bad thought and will result in disaster. Only by having a correct technique in the use of registers and resonators, and the accompanying control of breath pressure, compression and suppression, can the range of the voice be extended. The voice must be exercised on scales and arpeggi, gradually adding an extra note or notes. At first possibly nine-note scales, then adding an extra note until scales of one octave and five notes are easily accomplished. As security is developed, practise on such lines as follow may be undertaken. Naturally, practise must be undertaken in keys appropriate to individual voice categories.

If necessary a breath may be taken on the last tied note.

'WHAT TYPE OF VOICE DO I HAVE?'

CHAPTER FOURTEEN

'Rest' – the danger of overwork

Temporary trouble can occur by overwork or fatigue. One can push the voice into working when it should be resting. The wise young singer realises that sometimes one should say 'No, thank you' when the engagement book is becoming too heavily laden. This is very difficult, of course, and especially when the offer is for a work which one would very much like to perform.

Resting is a problem that must be faced. It is essential that time for rest is allowed for in a profession that makes great demands on both bodily stamina and nerves. Nowadays, with modern travel, it is possible to cover thousands of miles in a few days and this, together with the ensuing performances, make great demands, which could no doubt eventually have adverse effects on vocal standards. Don't let this happen – be wise and make provisions for REST in your timetable.

If you are ill, NEVER attempt to perform, especially if your throat is affected in any way. It is absolutely essential that you rest until recovery, otherwise great harm can be done to the voice and with ensuing waste of time.

CHAPTER FIFTEEN

Advice on the discovery of 'a voice'

In most cases the possibility of becoming a singer is not made apparent until a young person reaches the mature teens – usually at about the age of seventeen to nineteen. This applies especially to young males due to the complete change of vocal qualities which take place on reaching puberty. At this stage the vocal folds undergo changes, becoming thicker and tougher, giving the tone darker and more colourful qualities as the child voice disappears. As these changes are taking place in the earlier teens there should be a period of rest and no serious attempts to sing should be undertaken until the 'new' voice is settled. The young female voices show much less actual change in the teens, only becoming stronger with much more development in tonal ability and displaying more definite characteristics as to range and quality as the voice matures with training.

It is at this stage – that of discovering the possibility of a promising voice – that many young would-be singers may be faced with a serious problem. In many cases they will not have any musical knowledge and it must be made very clear to them what is entailed by this fact, if a decision is to be made as to whether or not to undertake serious voice training.

If one is to speak the language of music it is imperative that one must learn the grammar of that subject. This embodies all musical techniques, rudiments, harmony, sight-reading of music and aural training. Together with these, the study of diction, which should include some lessons in elocution and, most essentially, languages. Italian, German, French are 'musts', but *all* languages are useful, so there are no limitations in this field of knowledge.

Take heart, young aspiring singers, it is not nearly so hard as it reads! So long as study in these subjects is undertaken immediately, there will be plenty of time to accomplish, with good tuition, all that is required for a high standard of musical efficiency during the five or six years ahead, which is approximately the period of time that

GENERAL ADVICE

should be estimated for full vocal development. But be sure that you do not find yourselves, after a great deal of study and hard work on voice production, with only a well-developed and secure vocal technique. No matter how excellent and proficient this may be, it will be quite useless unless your musicianship is of the very high standard demanded of singers today. If you cannot meet such standards there is little hope for a career as a professional singer.

There have been occasions when students have experienced this sad state of affairs, having omitted to realize the absolute necessity of good musicianship, and have found themselves quite unable to attain their ambitions to become professional singers.

CHAPTER SIXTEEN

'How does it go?' –
The study and approach to performing

It can safely be said that all young singers at some time have asked the question 'How does it go?'.

'How it goes' entails the employment of all the fundamental aspects of what is meant by PERFORMANCE. These are necessary to achieve authority and conviction in expressing music and words in varied styles.

The singer is blessed with the wonderful added advantage over all other instrumentalists in the approach to interpretation ... WORDS! In commencing the study of any vocal composition the most obvious first step to be taken is to read the words *and* to understand them. By doing just that, one will be easily halfway to realizing the manner to employ in expressing them. To *understand* them he must, of course, know the language in which they are written or, by a really intelligent and accurate translation of them into his native tongue, become aware of their exact meaning. It is not always easy to find such translations, hence the encouragement of students to learn languages as an essential part of their training. It is necessary to emphasise the vital importance of the use of expert diction in all performances. Accurate and controlled articulation and clear, colourful pronunciation and the use of nuance and verbal expression are absolutely essential.

Also one must fully understand, through the study of the history of music, the manner and style of setting words to music used by composers in the various epochs of musical history; an awareness of the differences in musical styles of the composers will have great bearing on the authenticity and authority of interpretation in performances, and thus plays an important part in answering the question 'How does it go?'.

An example of the individuality and diversity of musical ideas of composers in setting words can be seen in the manner of approach which Vaughan Williams used in his settings of Fredegond Shove's poem *The New Ghost* and that of Robert Stevenson's *The Roadside Fire* from *Songs of Travel*.

In the first instance Vaughan Williams has created a serene, mystical atmosphere, beautifully depicting the raising of a soul and its meeting with its God, and, we presume, its journey into the unknown.

Here the movement of the music is very free, falling easily in speech rhythm – it is marked *Senza Misura*, thus giving the impression of having no binding bar-lines or demanding beats, but leaving complete freedom for verbal emphasis and punctuation, and literally telling the singer and accompanist to move in perfect sympathy with each other, having no feeling of any actual rhythmic ties. The voice floats above the accompaniment, which at times consists of sustained chords and at other times, gently flowing arpeggio passages. As the scene ends, the voice completely parts company with the accompaniment (the instruction for this to take place is given by the composer), which would seem to depict the ascension of the soul, and leaving the more earthy sound of the world behind in the closing bars of the accompaniment.

The *Roadside Fire* is a gently earnest love song set in the open air of the country-side. It describes the life-style of a young couple 'living rough'. The boy fashions brooches, trinkets and toys from natural resources, the girl cleans and cooks at the open fire. They sleep under the stars, awakening to the singing of the birds, as the boy sings a love-song known only to them. The words here are set to a very light, firm rhythmical movement, expressing all the gentle emotions of the lovers in a happy vocal line, accompanied by dancing, tripping arpeggi and chords. Just one example of two very contrasting styles from the pen of the same person.

Great contrasts are to be found in the setting of the same poem by different composers, and one can note the individual approach made by each one.

Take Shakespeare's poem *O Mistress Mine*, which has been set to music over and over again. Here are three settings, greatly contrasted in approach.

Quilter (published Boosey and Hawkes) has set them in a very gentle lyrical style, in a quiet moving manner, accompanied by chords and arpeggi, in which quite a deal of the vocal line is to be heard. It ends on a very gentle note for the final question, 'Where are you roaming?'.

Finzi (published Boosey and Hawkes in *Let Us Garlands Bring*) has made his accompaniment into a quick, dancing movement by using short groups of notes in a florid fashion for the right hand with a rocking staccato bass for the left hand. The voice part is very lively with quite a bit of syncopation and, again, some use of staccato, all of which goes to produce quite an agile type of song.

Norman Fulton's setting (OUP) was written for a radio performance of *Twelfth Night*. It has a very gentle, enquiring voice part of short phrases, the accompaniment being of quiet spread chords which give an impression of lute accompaniment. Generally speaking a small enchanting musical cameo.

Interpretation

A dictionary definition of the word 'interpretation' in connection with music is given as follows: 'The spirit of a piece of music in accordance with the performer's conception of it.'

There is no way in which it is possible for a composer to indicate his precise wishes as to an exact interpretation of his compositions. He can, and does, use musical symbols and words to indicate movement and style. He can state his wishes as to the phrasing and punctuation of both music and words. These are means by which he can make some of the ideas in his interpretation visible to the performers, who must pay faithful attention to them and always combine them in his own individual approach to interpretation. From these visual aids and instructions the singer must then, by a sensitive and intelligent study of the music and the words, seek an appreciation of the composer's ideas and thoughts in the composition. With his musical and poetic instinct and intention, the performer must sense what is contained in the piece and, with his own imaginative powers and conception, bring the spirit of the composition to life. Obviously the actual creation and interpretation of any form of art (in this case that of music) is a completely individual act on the part of the creator – here the composer; the singer is the means by which it is communicated to the listeners in a faithful endeavour to present it to them in the manner he feels to be the wishes of the composer. Unless very specific instructions as to the speed and tonal levels are given by the composer himself (not those inserted by editors or arrangers) it is necessary, and quite permissible, for the performer to make use of certain technical and expressive musical means to add his own ideas and insight to what he sees written in the score. However, special attention must be given to the style and period of the composition by knowledge of this aspect.

It is quite certain that the *movement* of music should never be just sounds which merely move up and down in pitch. There should be more of a feeling of curves in the movement, mounting and descending towards certain points of verbal and musical emphasis or climax which become instinctive in an accomplished performer. There should always be a forward impulse in the phrasing, the intention of 'going somewhere', a point to aim for, which is often a strong beat or word or syllable needing a definite stress or accent. One has sometimes heard the instruction to 'hold' a note in accordance with its value, but the longest notes ever sustained must still have the sense of movement, and in good singing always do – providing the singer has complete control of his breathing apparatus.

The tonal levels and various areas of resonance can be varied to induce emotions of excitement, repose, and so on, in both verbal and musical expression. However, it is generally accepted that from a musical point of view some slight increase in tone can be used in a rising phrase and, that having given this tonal lift, there can be a feeling of coming more to rest as a phrase descends, providing this is in agreement with word sense. These are all part of the technical means by which the performer is able to add his contributions to the expression; but they must always be directed by his musical and sensitive desires and used very judiciously.

Some comparisons and observations in the requirements and approach to the various areas of music may be made here, for instance, those of opera, oratorio, choral works and recital work.

Singers who find themselves possessed of the vocal attributes or qualities necessary for operatic singing will naturally wish to gravitate towards the opera stage. This will entail study of acting and knowledge of stage-craft under the guidance of a coach and theatrical producer. The role of the actor-singer is one in which tremendous opportunities of interpretation are to be found in the combination of singing and acting, for the united expression of both arts. For those who are successful in this direction, it will be found to be a medium which is unbounded in artistic and emotional possibilities.

Whilst the singers can make use of all the aids of stage-craft, together with guidance by producers, repetiteurs and musical directors, the main onus for success will lie on the individual, who must preserve his own identity in the roles undertaken and not find himself the victim of mere mimicry. Such undertakings demand great resources of character and obviously not all those who seek to achieve such ambitions will be successful. For those who *do* succeed, there is no doubt that it will prove a wonderful and rewarding experience.

In the performance of oratorio it should be accepted that it would be unwise to use this musical platform as a medium for acting: the actor-singer's place is rightly on the opera stage. Nevertheless, there is the necessity to *portray* their roles. Obviously there may be a spontaneous, almost subconscious movement or gesture from time to time which is quite understandable. However, for the most part, the singer must rely on nuance and his vocal and verbal powers of expression for the convincing portrayal of the characteristics of his roles. He is helped in this direction by the fact that nearly everyone is familiar with the arguments of works based on biblical and religious foundations. In secular works such as *Acis and Galatea* (Handel), the plots or stories are often to be found printed in the actual score, or can usually be discovered in musical encyclopaedias.

Facial expression is necessary in all performances (who wishes to be confronted with a dead-pan face?) but all contrived and artificial attempts to show one's feelings must be avoided. Unfortunately, certain present-day media exposure seems to encourage singers always to be trying to 'do something' in their presentations, resulting in extremes of so-called expression and facial contortions. If one sings with natural sincerity and real feeling for the content of the piece being performed, visual expression will be made quite subconsciously. It is quite possible to present a natural and relaxed appearance if all the technical, musical and artistic means which make up the art of singing are completely under the control of the performer.

Vocal powers must also be taken into consideration for the interpretation of various styles. For instance, for the most part one would not approach the interpretations of all lieder, English and French songs with the idea of demonstrating the size of one's voice, but, naturally, rather considering the perfection of artistry and understanding of the various qualities and styles required. However, this does not mean that voices do not have to respond in some cases to great vocal demands in such instances. Naturally, many songs of all

GENERAL ADVICE

nationalities call for great variety in tonal and dynamic scope and this must be judged by all and approached with musical and artistic discretion. On the other hand, in undertaking roles in opera or a part in big-scale works such as Verdi's *Requiem*, Beethoven's *Choral Symphony* and such like, it is necessary to have voices that can respond to the scope of the tonal demands made upon them.

Accompaniments

The importance of accompaniments as a vital part of any composition cannot be over-emphasised. They must be recognised as playing an equal proportion in the interpretation of music. A wise singer will know the accompaniment as well as he knows his vocal lines.

In the approach to this aspect of performance, let us take two songs written in very contrasted styles and compare the part that the accompaniment must play for their success in performance.

First, *Die Lorelei* by Liszt. This fine song, belonging to the romantic era, is a very descriptive vehicle embodying narrative, dramatic and emotional qualities. It is the mythological story of the siren-like woman called the Lorelei who inhabits the huge rock, the Lorelei Rock, which towers above a bend in the river Rhein in Germany. In the legend, the beautiful Lorelei sits high on the rock and as she combs her long golden hair, sings a glorious, sensual song. This attracts the curiosity of the Rhein boatmen, plying their trade up and down the river, who unwarily look above to see from whence the song comes. They do not see the dangers of the submerged rocks and the ever-changing conditions of the river; soon the boats are tossed and broken up and the boatmen are sent to their death. This is how the Lorelei works her plot of destruction. Here all the emotions and actions in the song are vividly illustrated in the accompaniment to the great vocal and expressive demands made on the singer.

The song opens with a few small detached chords which depict an errie atmosphere around the rock. This is followed by the entry of the voice in a short recitative in which the singer recalls the legend of the rock, and which will now be heard in the song.

The first section commences with very descriptive writing for the piano in establishing the general conditions around the rock. The smooth, seemingly gentle flow of the river, illustrated by warm, colourful chords and legato arpeggi passages, to accompany the line of the florid phrases in the voice part, emphasising height and depth. Suddenly there is a complete change. Sharp, strong and somewhat cruel repeated chords are heard, depicting the change in the waters as the boat approaches submerged rocks which are not seen by the inattentive boatmen, who are still entranced by the sight and sound of the Lorelei. Her singing now takes on a dramatic and sinister quality to give a portrayal of the tragedy which is about to take place.

This second section is full of frenzied musical emotion from both singer and accompaniment. The voice becomes very sinister in telling of the raging torrents which toss the helpless boatmen from their boat as it is destroyed by the turbulent waters. The latter is illustrated in the accompaniment by very fast repeated chords and big cadenza-like appeggi rising and falling. Both voice and accompaniment rise to a huge climax which then descends to a stillness, sinking, as do the unfortunate boatmen, to the depths of the river.

After a long pause, as the waters settle to a placid and smooth condition after the tragedy, the third section opens with a return to the style of the first section of the song, again depicting the Rhein in its gentle flowing motion. Here, the voice is telling us that part of the legend, 'this is what happens when the dreaded Lorelei works her sinister magic' from which, it seems, she derives some grim and heinous satisfaction.

The song ends with a gradual, long rising phrase for both voice and accompaniment, made to a long *diminuendo* and ending on a highly poised note in the top part of the voice, which sould seem to indicate the Lorelei returning to her place high on the rock, in preparation to repeat the everlasting act of destruction of unwary boatmen.

In comparison, one may look at a song like *Wohin*, the second song from the Schubert song-cycle *Die schöne Müllerin*, written in the classical-romantic style. Here, at first sight, the accompaniment might appear to be very simple and it might easily be thought to play only an insignificant part in the interpretation of the song. This would be erroneous. The accompaniment is the mainstay in illustrating the ever-lasting, babbling brook which plays an important part in the story of the fair maid of the mill. The rhythm is very strict — one could almost say monotonous — leaving little room for much expressive change in the movement, which in any case would be out of character.

GENERAL ADVICE

Another aspect of style in accompaniment is met with in the classical writing of that era. For instance, take the aria *Hark, hark the echoing air* from Purcell's *Fairy Queen*. Here the singer and the orchestral accompaniment must maintain a strict rhythm almost throughout the aria, which calls for great agility, leaving only very little possibility for any attempt of florid movement, which again would be out of character for the period.

At the latter part of study and the early part of a career, every effort should be made by singers to find a good accompanist. The importance of working regularly with such a partner cannot be over-emphasised. It is necessary in learning repertoire and roles and later to have an accompanist with whom a rapport has been established and on whom they can rely to support them in their performances.

In working regularly together, satisfactory and productive discussion is made possible between them as to the musical and poetic approach to be undertaken in the preparation of music which is proposed to be studied and performed. It is absolutely necessary that they are in agreement as to the musical markings and understanding of the poetry, so that the overall expression has their mutual relationship. There must be a finely drawn agreement on tempi, dynamics and general nuance, and a deep and thorough appreciation of the words in their various emotions and descriptive content. Singer and accompanist together must realize the musical and poetic content and, by instinct and intuition, carry out in their interpretation what they conceive to be the composer's wishes and intentions, using whatever indications are available. Great demands will be made in the performance of the English, German, French and Italian repertoire, both classical and contemporary in style. It is very doubtful whether such demands could be successfully met without the afore-mentioned understanding between singer and accompanist. Blest is the singer who has a good accompanist to aid him in his musical imagination and enterprise.

Be wise – be a good singer, but be sure to be a first-class musician too!

CHAPTER SEVENTEEN

Repertoire

From the very beginning of training the knowledge of repertoire must be considered as a most important part of a singer's study.

It behoves all young singers to prepare for that time when they will be called upon to perform all the types and styles of music which go to make up repertoire.

In preparation for the ultimate comprehensive repertoire for professional singers, knowledge of what follows will be expected, but naturally, individual choices will be made in selecting from the various categories:

1. The standard oratorios, choral works, and operas. British, German, French and Italian songs, including the great song-cycles and song collections of such composers as Schubert, Schumann and Wolf and many British and French composers.

2. The tremendous output of songs by composers before the nineteenth century should be studied and selections included in repertoire:

British composers: Byrd, Dowland, Campion, Morley, Rosseter, Tallis, Ford, Gibbons, Blow, Purcell, Leveridge, Carey, Arne, Boyce, Linley, Shield, etc.

Outstanding German and Austrian composers of this era include Schutz, Bach, Handel, Telemann, Gluck, Haydn, Mozart, amongst many others lesser known.

Pre-eminent French composers of this time include Lully, Charpentier, Campra, Couperin, Rameau, Grétry.

Songs by Italian composers, such as Caccini, Cherubini, Peri, Monteverdi, Carissimi, Torelli, Scarlatti, Vivaldi, Bononcini, Durante, Pergolesi, Paisiello, Caldara, Cimarosa, all of whom were pre-eminent in this period.

3. Following this period the 19th- and 20th-century songs and song-cycles of British, American, German and French composers are, of

REPERTOIRE

course, of the utmost importance in any singer's repertoire, as it is from these sources that recital programmes are mainly built.

The letters which appear after a composers name indicate song-cycles and/or song collections (SC), choral works involving solo voices (CH) and (O) for opera. There are, of course, solo songs by these composers in addition to these categories.

Pre-eminent among British and American composers are: Bantock, Bax, Berkeley (SC), Bliss, Bridge, Britten (SC, CH, O), Geoffrey Bush (SC), Butterworth (SC), Delius (CH), Elgar (SC, CH), Finzi (SC), Gurney (SC), Gibbs, Head, Holst, Howells, Ireland (SC), Moeran (SC), Parry, Quilter, Harty (SC, CH), Rubbra (SC), Shaw, Somervell (SC), Sullivan (O), Vaughan Williams (SC, CH, O), Warlock (SC), Walton (SC, CH), Barber, Bernstein (CH), Carpenter, Copland, Griffes, Hageman, Ives, Naginski, Menotti (CH, O), Rorem (CH).

Some more contemporary composers, mostly British, are Peter Racine Fricker, Thea Musgrave, Brian Dennis, John Joubert, Malcolm Williamson, Richard Rodney Bennett (SC), Alan Bush, William Mathias, Jonathan Harvey (CH), Henze, Priaulx Rainier (SC), Nicholas Maw (SC), Elisabeth Lutyens, William Alwyn, Robin Holloway, Roger Steptoe (SC, CH), Trevor Hold (CH), Michael Tippett (SC, O, CH), John Gardiner, Richard Stoker, Alun Hoddinott (CH), Michael Berkeley (CH) and Geoffrey Burgon (CH).

Also included should be the songs of Swiss-born Bloch (SC), and Honegger (SC, CH); the Czech composer Dvořák (CH, O); the Hungarians Liszt, Kodaly, Bartok; the Russian composers Borodin (O), Prokofieff, Tchaikovsky (O), Rimsky-Korsakof (CH, O), Rachmaninof (O), Stravinsky (CH, O); the Polish composers Chopin and Szymanowski; and those songs of the Scandinavians Grieg (Norway) and Sibelius (Finland).

Pre-eminent among German composers are: Beethoven (SC, CH), Berg (SC, O), Brahms (SC, CH), Franz, Hindemith (SC, CH), Löwe (famous for his ballads), Mahler (SC, CH), Mendelssohn (CH), Schönberg (CH), Schubert (SC) (who, together with Schumann and Wolf produced the most famous collections of songs and song-cycles of all time), Strauss (SC, O), Weber (SC, O), Webern (SC).

The most outstanding French composers are: Berlioz (SC, O), Bizet (O), Chabrier (SC), Chaminade (SC), Charpentier (SC, O), Chausson (SC), Debussy (SC): Duparc, Fauré (SC), Franck, Gounod

REPERTOIRE

(SC, O), Massenet (O), Messiaen (SC), Milhaud (SC), Poulenc (SC), Ravel (SC, CH), Saint-Saëns (SC, CH).

The output of Italian composers in this period is somewhat limited but the important songs of three eminent composers – Castelnuovo-Tedesco, Respighi and Pizzetti – should be included in repertoire. Other composers of note include the more contemporary writers Malipiero and Casella.

Obviously to accomplish even selections from such extensive and demanding repertoire will take many years of gradual study and general vocal development.

Needless to say, valuable knowledge is gained by attendance at opera and oratorio performances, recitals and concerts, and through tapes, recordings, and radio and TV programmes. The larger public libraries provide a music section from which scores may be borrowed and reference books consulted, and certain publishers have extensive song catalogues. From all these sources much knowledge and information concerning repertoire may be obtained. In addition, an invaluable publication on repertoire which can be highly recommended is *Music for the voice* – a descriptive list of concert and teaching material compiled by Sergius Kagen. It is published by Indiana University Press, Bloomington, London, USA.

It is not possible or desirable for any singer to undertake performance of every type of work. It should become quite apparent what is most suited to the individual's voice qualities as experience is gained. For instance, a lyrical voice will for the most part be happy in some of the roles in Mozart operas and the oratorios of Bach, Handel and Haydn. In contrast, it would not be wise to consider roles in the more dramatic operas of Verdi, Puccini, Strauss, etc, or to undertake a part in such works as Beethoven's *Choral Symphony*, Verdi's *Requiem*, Mahler's *Choral Symphony* or Rossini's *Stabat Mater*, all of which call for much more dramatic qualities and greater vocal stamina. However, it must be recognised that as voices mature, great changes take place and it is within the bounds of possibility that a lyrical voice may develop with experience and take on dramatic qualities which have not been apparent in earlier stages of training. This has happened many times.

In choosing songs in the early stages it is necessary to bear in mind that there will be limitations in various aspects of technique.

The phrasing must not be demanding. The speed must not be very slow or very fast. Compass will be restricted so that any piece needs to lie more or less in the medium register of the voice, and the movement should not entail big intervals. Tonal scope will also be limited; pieces which contain great variety in dynamics must therefore be avoided so as to ensure that the voice is not put to any strain. The poem or verses should not demand dramatic or over-emotional expression, as this might cause over-endeavour and strain; they should be as natural and 'everyday' as possible, gently descriptive, simple narrative, and so on.

The natural qualities of the voice as it is in this stage of training will also dictate the music suitable for the various stages of development, but generally speaking it should tend to the more lyrical in style; anything which avoids over-demanding use of the voice will be acceptable. On discovering evidence of strain on the voice by any particular piece, it must be put aside at once, perhaps for later consideration. For examples of suitable material for early stages of training and development, a suggested list is given later in this chapter.

Early limitations in practical work, however, should not restrict the full study of repertoire, the knowledge of which can be sought after, as it suggested, from the very beginning of training.

Now follow suggestions as to material suitable for the early stages of singing ability and vocal development and the progression towards more demanding pieces.

Material for the early stages of training and development

In the following pages the sole publisher of each song is normally indicated. Where it is not, the choice can be made from several available editions. In some cases the song is included in a song-cyle or song-set. In some cases the song is only available from the publisher in the form of an authorised photocopy.

For early stages of training, some well-chosen setting of folk-songs and traditional airs from the United Kingdom, arranged with interesting and pianistically conceived accompaniments, may be studied. Many such songs have been arranged by such composers as Quilter, Vaughan Williams, Somervell, Moffat, Hughes, Harty, Kennedy-Fraser, Sharp and Britten. For example:

REPERTOIRE

BH = Boosey and Hawkes   C = Chester   CR = Cramer
D = Ditson   N = Novello   SB = Stainer and Bell

English folksongs
Six English Folk Songs   Vaughan Williams (SB)
Drink to me only   Quilter (BH)
Over the Mountains   Quilter (BH)
The Sweet Nightingale   Sharp (N)
As down in the meadows   Sharp (N)
The Ashgrove   Britten (BH)
Early one morning   Britten (BH)

Scottish folksongs
An Eriskay love lilt
  from *Songs of the Hebrides*)   Kennedy Fraser (BH)
Coming through the rye   Hopekirk (D)
Loch Lomond   Hopekirk (D)
Speed bonny boat (Skye Boat
  Song)   Lawson (CR)
Turn ye to me   Reid (BH)

Irish folksongs
A Ballynure ballad   Hughes (BH)
I know where I'm going   Hughes (BH)
I will walk with my love   Hughes (BH)
She moved through the fair   Hughes (BH)
A gartan mother's lullaby   (Hughes (BH)
The gentle maiden   Somervell (BH)
My Lagan Love   Harty (BH)
The Fairy King's courtship   Harty (BH)

American folksongs
The little horses   Copland (BH)
At the River   Copland (BH)
Long time ago   Copland (BH)
Simple gifts   Copland (BH)
John Riley   Brockway (D)
I'm sad and I'm lonely   Sandburg (Harcourt, Brace)
Foggy foggy dew   Sandburg (Harcourt, Brace)
As I walked out   McGill (BH)
He's gone away   Downes (Harvell, Soskins)
Night-herding song   Downes (Harvell, Soskins)
Negro-spirituals   arr Burleigh (Belwin Mills)
Nobody knows de trouble I've seen
Steal away
Swing low, sweet chariot
Oh Peter, go ring-a dem bells
Heavn', Heav'n

REPERTOIRE

Some more demanding folksongs could well be considered later for inclusion in recital programmes, for instance:

Jamaican folksongs, arr Benjamin (BH)
Song of the banana carriers
Oh, what a Saturday night
French folksongs, arr Bax (C)
Seven Spanish folksongs, arr De Falla (C)
El pano moruno
Seguidilla Murciana
Asturiana
Jota
Nana
Cancion
Polo

There are also many other Spanish folksongs arranged by de Falla. Among them are transcriptions of old Spanish Christmas carols, *Vingt Chants Populaires Espagnol*, and also some Latin American songs.

Continuing with music suitable for early stages of training, the following list of suggested English songs may also be considered:

When daises pied	Arne (CR)
Now Phoebus sinketh in the west	Arne (CR)
Under the greenwood tree	Arne (CR)
Blow, blow thou winter wind	Arne (CR)
The song of Momus to Mars	Boyce (OUP)
Rail no more, ye learned asses	Boyce (OUP)
Angels ever bright and fair	Handel
Art thou troubled?	Handel
Silent worship	Handel
Droop not young lover	Handel
Sylvia, now your scorn	Purcell
Ah, how pleasant 'tis to love	Purcell
I attempt from love's sickness	Purcell
She never told her love	Haydn
My mother bids me bind my hair	Haydn
Trade winds	Keel (BH)
The cloths of heaven	Dunhill (SB)
How soft upon the evening air	Dunhill (Curwen)
Dream valley	Quilter (BH)
Spring sorrow	Quilter (BH)
O mistress mine	Quilter (BH)
Through the sunny garden	Quilter (BH)
The shepherd's song	Elgar (Thames)

REPERTOIRE

The sky above the roof	Vaughan Williams (BH)
Linden lea	Vaughan Williams (BH)
Bright is the ring of words	Vaughan Williams (BH)
Hymn to the virgin	Rubbra (Lengnick)
A melancholy song	Hopkins (Chester)
If there were dreams to sell	Ireland (BH)
Sea fever	Ireland (BH)
The countryman	Warlock (BH)
I know a bank	Shaw (BH)
Sweet chance	Head (BH)
A soft day	Stanford (BH)

Useful collections of English songs are:

A Tuneful Voice, 25 classical English songs, edited by Timothy Roberts (OUP)
The Singer's Collection, Vols 1 and 2, edited by Alan Ridout (Kevin Mayhew)
A Heritage of 20th Century British Song, in four volumes (Boosey and Hawkes)
The Cramer Song Folio, Vols 1 and 2 (Cramer)
One Hundred English Folksongs, edited by Cecil Sharp (Dover)
Songs of England, edited by Hargest-Jones (Boosey and Hawkes)
A Century of English Song (Thames)
Stainer and Bell publish an extensive series of English song volumes, as do Thames Publishing.

Another useful source for development in the early stages of training is some of the less demanding songs by 17th- and 18th-century Italian composers — 'Arie Antiche' — such as:

Caro mio ben	Giordani
Vittorio, mio core!	Carissimi
Sebben, crudele	Caldara
Per la gloria d'adorarvi	Bononcini
Tu lo sai	Torelli
Nel cor più non mi sento	Paisiello

The Associated Board publishes a selection of *Italian Arias 1600–1800*, edited by Anthony Lewis, and Schirmer publish *24 Italian Songs and Arias of the 17th and 18th Centuries*.

Two other series to be considered are the three volumes of *Celebrated Songs*, selected and graded for the developing voice by Shirley Leah (Chester) and the *Sing Solo* series, five volumes (one for each main voice-type, plus one Christmas volume), with John Carol Case as general editor (OUP).

REPERTOIRE

Material suitable for further development

As further singing technique is developed and accomplished, some carefully chosen arias from oratorio and even perhaps opera — for example those given below — could now be considered, but the young singer must still bear in mind the previous advice given concerning limitations on technique and the danger of over-stressing the vocal instrument at relatively early stages of training.

Publishers are not given as in almost every case there are alternative editions from which to choose.

SOPRANO
Secular and sacred oratorio:
As when the Dove (*Acis and Galatea*)	Handel
Come unto Him (*Messiah*)	Handel
Ye men of Gaza (*Judas Maccabeus*)	Handel
Jesus Saviour, I am thine (*St Matthew Passion*)	Bach
Pie Jesu (*Requiem*)	Fauré

Opera:
Batti, batti, o bel Massetto (*Con Giovanni*)	Mozart
Vedrai carino (*Don Giovanni*)	Mozart
Un moto di gioia (*Le nozze di Figaro*)	Mozart

MEZZO/CONTRALTO
Secular and sacred oratorio:
Eia Mater (*Stabat Mater*)	Pergolesi
He shall feed his flock (*Messiah*)	Handel
O rest in the Lord (*Elijah*)	Mendelssohn

Opera:
Non so piu (*Le nozze di Figaro*)	Mozart
Voi che sapete (*Le nozze di Figaro*)	Mozart

TENOR
Secular and sacred oratorio:
Thy rebuke has broken his heart (*Messiah*)	Handel
But Thou didst not leave his soul (Messiah)	Handel
In native worth (*Creation*)	Haydn
Shepherd, what art thou pursuing? (*Acis and Galatea*)	Handel
Now Phoebus sinketh in the west	Arne

Opera:
Come' e gentil (*Don Pasquale*)	Donizetti
M'appari (*Martha*)	Flotow

REPERTOIRE

BARITONE/BASS
Secular and sacred oratorio:
How willing my paternal love (Samson)	Handel
Shall I in Mamres' fertile plain (Joshua)	Handel
More sweet is that name (Semele)	Handel
Leave me loathsome light (Semele)	Handel
The Saviour low before his father bending (St Matthew Passion)	Bach
'Twas in the cool of eventide (St Matthew Passion)	Bach
At evening, hour of calm and peace (St John Passion)	Bach
Quia fecit mihi magna (Magnificat)	Bach

Opera:
Si trai ceppi (Berenice)	Handel
Deh vieni alla finestra (Don Giovanni)	Mozart
Non piu andrai (Le nozze di Figaro)	Mozart
In diesen heilgen Hallen (Zauberflöte)	Mozart
O Isis und Osiris (Zauberflöte)	Mozart

Useful books

The Concert Song Companion – a guide to the classical repertoire, Charles Osborne (Gollancz).
A History of Song, Denis Stevens (Hutchinson).
Introduction to the Art Song, Barbara Meister (Taplinger).
New Vocal Repertory, Jane Manning (Macmillan).
The Art of Auditioning, Anthony Legge (Rhinegold).
British Music Yearbook (Rhinegold).
Lieder line by line and word for word, Lois Phillips (Duckworth).
The Penguin Book of Lieder, S S Prawer (Penguin).
The Fischer-Dieskau Book of Lieder, Dietrich Fischer-Dieskau (Gollancz).
German Song and its Poetry 1740–1900, J W Smeed (Croom Helm).
Lieder – an introduction to German Song, Kenneth Whitton (Julia MacRae).
Poem and Music in the German Lied from Gluck to Hugo Wolf, Jach Stein (Harvard University Press).
Singing in French – a manual of French diction and French song repertoire, Thomas Grubb (Collier Macmillan).
Interpretation of French Song, Pierre Bernac (Gollancz).
Nineteenth Century French Song, Barbara Meister (Indiana University Press).
French Song from Berlioz to Duparc, Frits Noske (Dover).
Arie Antiche, English translations by Dorothy Richardson and Tina Ruta (Paraclete Press).
Diction – Italian, Latin, French, German ... the sounds, and 81 exercises for singing them, John Moriaty (E C Schirmer).
English Solo Song – guides to the repertoire, Michael Pilkington (Thames Publishing).

REPERTOIRE

Useful organisations

Association of Teachers of Singing, The Sideways House, 146 Greenstead Road, Colchester CO1 2SN (0206 867462)
Association of English Singers and Speakers, 25 Tamar House, Kensington Lane, London SE11 4XA (071 582 1746)
Incorporated Society of Musicians, 10 Stratford Place, London W1N 9AE (071 629 4413)
British Music Information Centre, 10 Stratford Place, London W1N 9AE (071 449 8567)
Central Music Library (Westminster), 160 Buckingham Palace Road, SW1W 9UD (071 798 2192)